Gundel's Hungarian Cookbook

Gundel's Hungarian Cookbook

Corvina Kiadó

Title of the original: *Kis magyar szakácskönyv,* Corvina Kiadó, 1984
Translated by Ágnes Kádár
Translator's adviser: J. Audrey Ellison

© The estate of Károly Gundel, 1956
ISBN 963 13 2623 3

The photographs were taken by János Huschit.
The objects seen on the photographs are from the Museum of Hungarian Commerce and Catering
(Budapest I., Fortuna utca 4)
The dishes seen on the photographs were made by Márton Jung,
who was a Gundel cook for 40 years, and cook Sándor Tréfás
On the cover: Steak à la Feszty

Contributors to the original edition: Károly Márk, Chef of the former Crown Prince István Hotel
under János Gundel's management, János Rákóczi, Chef of the Hotel Gellért Restaurant under
Károly Gundel's management, Elek Rehberger, Chef of the Gundel Restaurant in the Budapest
City Park

Design: László Tasnádi
Thirteenth edition

Printed in Hungary, 1988
Kner Printing House, Békéscsaba
CO 2631-h-8890

Contents

❖ Contents ❖

Contents

Contents

Contents

1.
A Word from the Publisher

This book was first published in 1934 in German, then in English and French; a few of the recipes were even translated into Japanese, to encourage the use of paprika in Japan. Subsequently, it was published in Hungarian, and after the author's death came the publication in Russian, Czech and Italian. Recently there were German and English editions in minibook form.

The 38 various editions proved the book's great success among culinary professionals and the general public.

The reason for this revised edition is best expressed by Escoffier in the introduction of his "Le guide culinaire" (published in 1907) where he wrote:

"We must accept the fact that lifestyles and customs have changed considerably since 1850, so that culinary art must also change with the times. The important works of Carême, Dubois and Bernard reflected the customs of their age, and are valued as such. However, in general, their books do not meet today's requirements. We may respect, study, and indeed even love these books, but we should not copy them. We must find new methods which will fit today's customs and practices..." Fifty years have passed since the first edition of Károly Gundel's cookbook. Eating and cooking habits have drastically changed in this time interval. As in other areas of consumer life, technological advances in the method of food preparation were very rapid. The food industry is constantly creating new products with new tastes. The upsurge of foreign visitors to Hungary helped us to discover which of our national foods are more or less acceptable to the international palate. Last but not least, an important reason for a revised edition is our readers' helpful suggestions.

This completely revised edition was written by Károly Gundel's two sons, Ferenc and Imre, worthy successors to their famous father. The late Ferenc Gundel was an Associate Professor at the High School of Catering; Imre is an Associate of the Museum of Catering. At the request of Ferenc and Imre Gundel, we are including a short biography of Károly Gundel, since 1983 was the 100th anniversary of his birth. The Hungarian People's Republic honored Károly Gundel's achievements in the culinary field and in the tourist trade, and showed that it valued his character by retaining the Gundel name over his restaurant even after the 1949 Nationalization Act.

★ ★ ★ ★

8

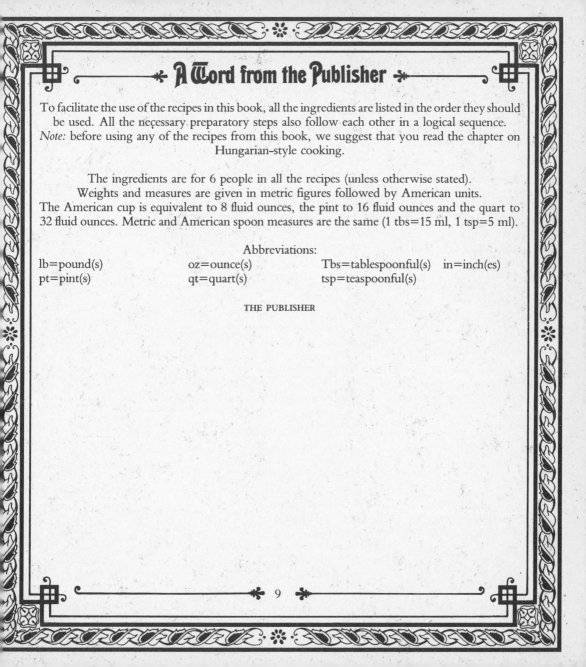

❋ A Word from the Publisher ❋

To facilitate the use of the recipes in this book, all the ingredients are listed in the order they should be used. All the necessary preparatory steps also follow each other in a logical sequence. *Note:* before using any of the recipes from this book, we suggest that you read the chapter on Hungarian-style cooking.

The ingredients are for 6 people in all the recipes (unless otherwise stated).
Weights and measures are given in metric figures followed by American units.
The American cup is equivalent to 8 fluid ounces, the pint to 16 fluid ounces and the quart to 32 fluid ounces. Metric and American spoon measures are the same (1 tbs=15 ml, 1 tsp=5 ml).

Abbreviations:

lb=pound(s)   oz=ounce(s)   Tbs=tablespoonful(s)   in=inch(es)
pt=pint(s)   qt=quart(s)   tsp=teaspoonful(s)

THE PUBLISHER

2.
A Short Biography

(Budapest: Sept. 23, 1883–Nov. 28, 1956)

Gundel was a simple, honest innkeeper who loved his profession, liked people in general, and adored his family.

The Gundel name is as renowned in Budapest as Sacher in Vienna, Horcher in Madrid, and Kempinski in Berlin. The American gastronome Joseph Wechsberg in *Blue Trout and Black Truffle* compared him with Escoffier and Fernand Point. His father, János Gundel, was the president of

the Hotel, Restaurant and Innkeepers' Association for 35 years. For a time he ran the Crown Prince István Hotel. This is where Károly, still a schoolboy, started to learn the trade which made the Gundel name world famous. At 23, after completing his foreign education, Károly began to work as an assistant in Tátralomnic at the Wagon Lits Hotel. Within 2 years he became the manager of the hotel. After his marriage he leased the restaurant at the City park (Zoo) in Budapest. He had this lease from 1910 until the nationalization of the restaurant in 1949. He also ran the restaurants of the Royal Hotel from 1920 to 1925, and the restaurants of the St. Gellért Hotel from 1927 to 1948.

On the Gundel menus, besides the Hungarian and French specialities, one could regularly find the culinary creations of Károly Gundel. He used Hungarian and imported ingredients. Seasonal specialities were always first available in the Gundel restaurants. In the 1930s his wine list contained 300 items, including 1811 vintage Tokay wine and foreign specialities.

His days were similar to that of other restaurateurs. In the morning he marketed at the large city market and did some office work, then checked on personnel at the Hotel Gellért. During the noon and evening hours he greeted the customers, first at the Hotel Gellért restaurant, than at the City Park (Zoo) restaurant. In his "free" time he read the professional literature to which he also generously contributed. For decades he rarely took a day off.

The customers, whom he greeted in his amiable polite manner in both restaurants, came from all walks of life. The guests included politicians of the various parties, artists, lawyers, writers, scientists or storekeepers and tradesmen: the working people of the city. He considered himself a "Hungarian host, not an innkeeper who sells food and drink for money, but one who receives respected guests in his house." Next to a good host always stands a good hostess. It was also true in the case of Károly Gundel. His wife was an ideal helpmate who was not only a good mother to their 13 children, but with her good taste and keen business sense helped and encouraged her husband for almost 50 years. One of the reasons for their successful business was the loyalty of their employees: some of them worked for the Gundel enterprises for 20–30 years.

In the years between the First and Second World Wars, Károly Gundel played a leading role in the Hotel and Restaurant Owners' Association. He greatly contributed to international acceptance of the Hungarian cuisine and helped to increase the flow of tourists to Hungary.

We would like to mention a few of his books such as the *Small Hungarian Cookery Book* and *The Development of the Hungarian Kitchen and Cookbooks through the 18th Century*. He also collaborated with Frigyes Karinthy, one of the most gifted Hungarian writers of the 20th century, on a book for amateur hosts, *How to Be a Host and How to Be a Guest*. This successful book was revised for

❖ A Short Biography ❖

the professional restaurateur and published under the title, *The Art of Being a Host and Hosting as an Art* (all books in Hungarian).

Fate wasn't kind to Károly Gundel. Most of his property wealth was lost during the Second World War; by 1948 he was blind, and later contracted cancer. Even in his declining years he was proud that his name remained on the restaurant which he previously owned. He considered it to be an honor, like "having your statue unveiled while you are still alive".

He never mentioned, but certainly knew, that he deserved the honor. He had worked for it long and hard.

3.
From the Writings of Károly Gundel

It is with diffidence that I offer this small book to the friends of the Hungarian kitchen. I must admit I am not offering what I would prefer, a complete and clear picture of today's Hungarian cuisine. I can give you only the description of a few typical Hungarian dishes, and some of the specialities of my house. I would like to offer some advice for this and future generations. For the present: to have a variety of enjoyable dishes on the table. For the future: those who will be interested in the art of cooking and baking, could learn or smile at my attempts.

Today's Hungarian cuisine is a far cry from the one our ancestors carried over the Carpathian mountains a millennium ago. The typical Hungarian dishes are not even the same as they were a hundred or two hundred years ago. Modern Hungarian cuisine however does carry the traces of the ancient past: some of the dishes of today are similar to those enjoyed in remote Asia, where the Magyar tribes originated.

During the age of the Great Migration, the Magyar tribes lived the life of nomads. We presume that in their semi-permanent encampments they prepared and preserved some kind of food to be used during their wanderings. It is widely believed that today's *tarhonya*[1] is a descendant of the sundried pasta of the ancient past. Not only the Hungarian shepherds, who still enjoy this food, but people in the Caucasian mountains, in Mongolia, Iran and on the Balkan peninsula also use a similar name for this filling dish (Tarana, Tarkhana).

We also inherited our *bogrács* from our nomad ancestors. It is a cooking cauldron which can be hung over an open-air fire. Without doubt the ancient Magyars cooked in this bogrács food which is similar to today's *gulyás*.[2] This custom did not disappear when the migrating tribes settled down. Even today, the bogrács is a frequently used cooking utensil.

After the establishment of Hungary, a large variety of foreign influences helped the development of our national cuisine. The Italian wife of King Matthias and her retinue affected the Hungarian cuisine in the Middle Ages.

Later the most important influence came from the Turkish occupation. After the stunning defeat on the battlefield at Mohács in 1526, Turkey occupied a large portion of the country and held it for 150 years. Interestingly, this influence is not noticeable in Transylvanian cooking, which preserved its national character and remained free from foreign influence.

❈ From the Writings of Károly Gundel ❈

At about the same time the effects of French cuisine were also introduced through the Royal Court of Vienna. This influence became predominant in the second half of the 19th century in the fast developing restaurant and hotel trade.

Due to these historical developments Hungarian cuisine lost its original heaviness but kept its characteristic taste which was enhanced by the use of paprika. The products of the Hungarian kitchen became more refined, adapted to cosmopolitan tastes and reached world fame.

The soil, climate, and geography of Hungary can supply all the variety of food and drink one can imagine. The rivers Danube and Tisza and Lake Balaton offer several kind of delectable fish not found in Western Europe, and which are considered to be delicacies. The most famous fish is called *fogas* (Lucioperca lucioperca), the giant pike-perch from the pike-perch family. Similar fish exist in other rivers and lakes of Europe. But the variety from Lake Balaton, because of less environmental stress, has whiter and lighter meat and superior flavor. Young *fogas* under 1–1,5 kg (2–3 lb) is called *süllő* (pike-perch). Fish from our rivers are not far behind in quality, for example sturgeon. Other fresh-water fish often used are the catfish, carp and pike. Most of the fish are still alive when they reach the kitchens of our restaurants.

Among the appetizers goose liver is noteworthy. In Hungary the goose is force-fed to fatten it. As a result of this feeding method the liver becomes enlarged and light colored. The taste of it is excellent when served either hot or cold.

I also would like to direct attention towards our roast sucking pig. It is roasted crisp and rose-red and served much more often than in Western Europe. Hot and cold pork roast and jellied cold pork are favorites. Among game, hare, venison, wild boar, pheasant and quail often appear on the menu. The country is rich in poultry and the Hungarian turkey is world famous.

Words are inadequate to describe the variety and quality of Hungarian fruits. Peaches, apricots and Hungarian grapes are superior, and the taste of our melons is a revelation to a foreigner.

Besides lard, onion and paprika, a characteristic ingredient of the modern Hungarian cuisine is sour cream.

The following information on the use of paprika might come as a surprise to the reader. Paprika, which is considered to be the Hungarian national spice, was not generally known or used until the 19th century. In cookbooks published 200 years ago we find no mention of it; even those which were published in the early part of the 19th century barely suggest the use of paprika.[3] The pepper plant (Capsicum annuum) arrived to Europe in the 16th century. Probably it came from both East and West. This was the time of the Turkish conquest of Hungary. Turks grew the Eastern spice for their own household use. This theory of the origin of Hungarian paprika is supported by the

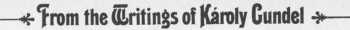

fact that the peppers grown in Spain are different from those grown in Hungary or on the Balkan peninsula. The Spanish pepper (pimiento) is similar to the one grown in South and Central America. It is large and meaty but has no special aroma. The type grown in Hungary is smaller and has a typical aroma, even the ones which are not hot.

Today *paprika* is the Hungarian national spice. Don't be scared of it. It might look red hot but good paprika doesn't taste violently hot. A large variety[4] is available today. The kind used in the better kitchens is bright red, slightly sweet and slightly hot. It is a unique spice. It is not hotter than the commonly used black pepper, in fact it is milder than spices like cayenne pepper and curry which are often used in England and America.

Actually, there are two kinds of peppers grown in Hungary: one for eating fresh, the other for spice. Peppers grown for eating fresh are green or yellow at first and later in the season turn red. Green and yellow pepper, which has a refreshing taste, is mostly consumed raw or in salads. It is a basic ingredient in a large variety of Hungarian dishes. The spice variety of pepper when red ripe is dried and pulverized to make paprika.[5] The quality and classification of the paprika depends on the variety of peppers used and on the proportion of the flesh, seeds and ribs mixed together in the processing plant.

In the Hungarian kitchen, as I mentioned previously, we often use sour cream. Originally this was skimmed from the top of *sour milk,* while sweet cream is from the top of *fresh milk.* In some of the better kitchens the use of sour cream is replaced by the use of heavy cream.

Quite a few recipes call for the use of fresh tomatoes and green peppers. When these are not available one can substitute tomato sauce or paste or a preserved tomato–green pepper mixture, called *lecsó* in Hungarian.

Outside Hungary most dishes prepared with paprika are called *gulyás.* But *gulyás* in Hungary is an entirely different dish. The Hungarian restaurants strive toward a uniform designation of dishes made with paprika. But in the provinces these uniform names are not always followed and the local designation could be different. There are four basic dish-groups which use paprika:

Gulyás: prepared with onion and paprika, contains cubed potato and small bits of dough (*csipetke*), and is a *soup-like* dish.

Pörkölt: more like a stew. Chopped onion is used to a greater extent and the gravy is thicker and richer.

Paprikás: an elegant *pörkölt.* White meat is used, less onion and less paprika flavor it. On the other hand the addition of sour cream or a mixture of sour and sweet cream produces a smoother gravy.

Tokány: similar to *pörkölt* or *paprikás,* however the meat is not cubed but cut in thin strips. Paprika

often loses its dominant role: black pepper and marjoram will be used more extensively; also bacon, sausage or mushrooms and green peas may be used to add flavor.

One of the typical Hungarian dishes which does not fit into these four categories is *Székely gulyás*. It is a stew made out of pork, flavored with paprika and sour cream and cooked with sauerkraut. Most of the dishes described in this book would not be very easy to digest. One should use good judgement, especially if the dinner guests are not all Hungarians. The Hungarian dishes should be interspersed with lighter fare. The variety will then make an interesting eating experience.

With these comments, I send this little book on its way. I am sure it will be a source of pleasure for those who use it and those who will enjoy the results. I strongly recommend a visit to Hungary to taste and savor the Hungarian flavors.

You are all welcome. Along with our excellent cuisine, the visitor should taste the wines of Badacsony, Eger and Tokaj. Listen and try to understand the gypsy music, our thousand years of history, our present-day problems and achievements.

I wish to all success and a good appetite!

KÁROLY GUNDEL

[1] *Tarhonya* is made out of egg dough, and has the size and shape of rice (see Recipe 90). Its equivalent in the U.S. is *egg barley*.

[2] The *gulyás* of bygone days did not contain potato, tomato or green pepper. In the 9th century the Byzantine army was fed from its herd of cattle which followed the marching army and slowed down its progress. The Magyar tribes' fighters were horsemen. The horses carried pasta, dried meat and dried milk *(hurut)*. When these horsemen reached water, they boiled water and poured it on the dried food, producing a nourishing meal.

[3] According to recent research, the planting and growing of peppers in vegetable gardens started in the 17th century. The use of red paprika did not begin until about 1748. According to some sources the grinding of red peppers to paprika was a Hungarian invention. In an 1830 cookbook the recommendation still was the use of pepper in fisherman's soup, not ground paprika.

[4] The official designation of the different varieties of paprika is in descending order of fineness: special *(különleges)*, mild *(csípősségmentes)*, delicate *(csemege)*, fine-sweet *(édes-nemes)*, semi-sweet *(féléedes)*, rose-red *(rózsa)*, hot *(erős)*. (See chapter IV. for more information.)

[5] In the recipes of this book we are going to refer to the fresh produce as *green pepper,* to the spice as *paprika.*

4.

About Hungarian-style Cooking

If you want to reproduce the authentic flavor of Hungarian dishes you must use real Hungarian lard, green pepper, paprika, tomato and onion. However, this is not always possible.

You can't obtain the same flavor if you use butter, oil or margarine instead of lard. Even if you are using *lard,* make certain it was produced by a higher temperature frying process and not by steam melting. The fragrance of onion will be enhanced by the fried flavor of the lard.

Lard is also the perfect medium for preserving the natural color of *paprika.* However, do not put paprika into overheated lard; it will produce a bitter taste and the color will be brown instead of red.

If the recipe calls for "special" (különleges), "delicate" (csemege) or "fine-sweet" (édes-nemes) paprika, do not worry about the seemingly excessive amount of it in the ingredient list; it is necessary to obtain the proper flavor. Of course one can experiment with a lesser amount of paprika. The hot or rose-red (erős, rózsa) paprika is used to add color and flavor *after* cooking. (In the recipes, paprika always means fine-sweet paprika.)

A dish might become spicy-hot because the *green pepper* used was hot. Test the green peppers before use by tasting the ribs; most of the spicy-hot chemical capsicine is located in the ribs and seeds of the green pepper. Even a very hot green pepper can be rendered "painless" by the removal of the ribs and seeds.

Red paprika not only gives a pleasant taste and color, but also contains vitamins A and C and is beneficial for the digestive system. It is one of the most versatile of spices. For example, before broiling fish or meat, dip it into a mixture of flour and paprika, this will give a finer texture and a superior taste.

If fresh *tomato* is not available, be careful when you substitute a canned product for it. Tomato paste in excess will produce a sweetish taste and ruin the character of most dishes. *If fresh tomato and green pepper are not available, 140 g (1 cup) green pepper and 60 g (¼ cup) tomato can be replaced by 100 g (7 Tbs) Hungarian canned lecsó, a mixture of stewed tomato and green pepper.*

We recommend mixing the *sour cream* half and half with heavy cream. This will produce a refined flavor but maintain the piquant sourness of the sour cream.

✳ About Hungarian-style Cooking ✳

Synthetic *food flavoring substances* are popular today. The use of these is a matter of preference. In this cookbook they are not even mentioned.

In reference to the *fish dishes:* almost any kind of fish can be used in our recipes. After all, there is not much chance that Hungarian fish is available. So substitute white-meat fish for pike (fogas) or trout, and dark-meat fish for carp or sturgeon.

✳ ✳ ✳ ✳

The thickening agent for most Hungarian soups and vegetables is a browned *roux*. Roux are not only used for thickening but also to add a characteristic flavor to some of the dishes. The use of a roux is also important if you want to use the water-soluble vitamins and minerals which are leached from the vegetables and discarded with the cooking water when vegetables are just boiled in the French or English manner of cooking. When a roux is used, the nourishing stock is thickened and served with the vegetables.

The roux is prepared by mixing flour into the hot, but not burning hot, shortening: use lard or butter for this purpose. The flour is browned over moderate heat while it is constantly stirred for a few seconds for a white roux; for a few minutes for a light or rose colored roux; and if the recipe calls for a dark or brown roux, the addition of a small amount of sugar and use of longer time will produce the dark brown color. When the roux has reached the proper color, add the required liquid (water, milk, consommé, a stock from the vegetables), *cold,* to the *hot* roux; stir it until it has a smooth texture; then add it to the food being prepared.

Before the liquid is added to the roux, a variety of spices and herbs could also be added and browned together. For example, in the preparation of a light roux for tender green peas, one can add parsley or red paprika or dill; in the case of a light brown roux for fresh bean soup, the addition of finely chopped onion, a small amount of garlic or paprika is recommended. Savoy cabbage requires a darker brown roux; onion, garlic or paprika will flavor it nicely. With squash (vegetable marrow) we use a light roux and the dominant herb is dill, but a small amount of finely chopped onion will enhance the flavor. For green beans, the primary flavoring of the light brown roux comes from garlic, but parsley and paprika can also be added.

Don't use too much flour in the roux, rather less than more. The liquid should barely cover the vegetables. Otherwise you will get an unappetizing gluelike substance with some vegetables floating in it. If you find before serving that the sauce is too thick, a small amount of water, milk or other liquid can be used to thin it. If, on the other hand, the sauce is too thin, mix flour with cold sour cream and add it to the sauce and vegetables. It will correct the consistency of the thin sauce.

❈ About Hungarian-style Cooking ❈

How to brown onion and use paprika

Chop the recommended quantity of onion very fine, then sauté it in the premelted lard (shortening). After sautéing, brown the onion to the color required for the dish being prepared. It requires some practice to get the proper color of the onion consistently. Because different onions contain different amounts of water, timing is not very practical. You must use your judgement, but the taste of the dish depends considerably on the color of the fried onion.

The color of the finished onions could be: blanched or translucent, pale yellow, golden yellow or light brown. When the proper color is reached the heat must be turned as low as possible; then immediately stir in the paprika, add the meat or vegetable (e.g.: mushrooms), and salt, and keep on stirring and browning. This process will take 3 to 4 minutes. Do not shorten this time: the typical taste of *pörkölt* comes from this method of roasting. (Roasted meat is not exactly the same as *pörkölt,* because a different technique is used in the browning of the meat.) Do not try to speed up the browning process by overheating the shortening: the paprika will acquire a dark color and will be bitter to the taste. While stirring the browning meat, add a small amount of water or some other liquid as necessary. This will also govern the temperature of the dish being prepared.

One last word

Since Hungarians, and indeed, all countries on the Continent, use the metric system of measurement, the recipes in this book are given in the metric system first, followed by close American approximations. Use whichever you prefer, just try not to mix them in your cooking!

Also, please note!
UNLESS OTHERWISE STATED, ALL INGREDIENTS ARE FOR 6 PERSONS.

5.
Soups

The recipes are for 3–4 dl (1¼–1¾ cups) portions per person. This is suitable for a 2–3 course meal. If a soup is used as a main course the quantities should be increased accordingly. If the soup is only an appetizer, served in cups, the quantities of the ingredients should be reduced, and chopped more finely to make the serving and eating more convenient. Serving Gulyás or Fisherman's soup in individual or family size *bogrács* gives an authentic air to the table setting.

Whenever possible use stock instead of water in the preparation of vegetables, gravy, sauce and soup; it gives a superior flavor. To prepare the stock use veal or beef bones, wash them well, cover them with cold water in a large pot and slowly simmer for 2 hours, then add soup vegetables and spices. (In the absence of stock, bouillon cubes may be used.)

We start out with the two basic soups, Gulyás and Fisherman's soup, and their variants.

1.
Gulyás Soup

360 g (2½ cups) cubed beef	800 g (1¾ lb) potato
80 g (5 Tbs) lard	140 g (1 cup) green pepper
150 g (⅞ cup) onion	60 g (1 small) fresh tomato
15 g (1 Tbs) paprika	6 portions of soup pasta
salt, garlic, caraway seeds	(csipetke, see Recipe 14)

Except for the proportions of the ingredients, this soup is prepared like Bográcsgulyás (Recipe 3).

2.
Mock Gulyás Soup

Substitute 500–600 g (1–1¼ lb) bones for the meat in the Gulyás soup recipe, and you'll get an inexpensive, tasty soup.

3.
Bográcsgulyás

1 kg (2¼ lb) beef	1 kg (2¼ lb) potato
80 g (5 Tbs) lard	140 g (1 cup) green pepper
300 g (1¾ cups) onion	60 g (1 small) fresh tomato
20 g (4 tsp) paprika	6 portions of soup pasta
salt, caraway seeds, garlic	(csipetke, Recipe 14)

Use meat rich in gelatine (shin-beef, blade or neck). Cube the meat into 1.5–2 cm (½–¾ in) pieces. Fry the chopped onion in the melted lard (shortening) until it is golden yellow. Lower the heat, then add the paprika, stir it rapidly, add the meat, keep on stirring, add salt. When the meat is browned and all the liquid is evaporated, add the caraway seeds, finely chopped garlic and a small amount of cold water, cover, and braise the meat slowly. Stir it occasionally and add small quantities of water if necessary. The meat should be braised, not boiled. While the meat is cooking, cube the potatoes, green pepper and tomatoes into pieces 1 cm (⅓ in) in size and prepare the dough for the soup pasta (csipetke). Just before the meat is completely tender, reduce the pan juices, add the cubed potatoes, let them brown slightly, add the stock, green pepper and tomato. When the potato is almost cooked and the soup is ready to be served, add the pasta (csipetke), and adjust quantity by the addition of stock or water.

4.
Bográcsgulyás Variations

Once the aspiring cook masters bográcsgulyás, the variations will become very easy, and not much explanation is needed at this point.

4/a. Gulyás à la Szeged and Gulyás Hungarian Plain Style: Reduce the potatoes in Recipe 3 to 700 g (1½ lb), and add 250 g (2 cups) mixed vegetables to the soup. For Gulyás Hungarian Plain Style, just omit the soup pasta (csipetke).

4/b. Serbian Gulyás: Omit the soup pasta from Recipe 3. Use only 600 g (1¼ lb) potatoes, and add 600 g (1¼ lb) Savoy cabbage cut in small segments.

❖ Soups ❖

4/c. Bean Gulyás: Omit the potatoes and caraway seeds from Recipe 3. Instead, use 350 g (2 cups) of soaked kidney beans when adding the meat to the soup.

4/d. Mutton Gulyás: Instead of beef use 1.5 kg (3¼ lb) of mutton; breast, ribs, neck, or shinmeat are all good for this soup. Remove the large bones. Small ones can be left with the meat. If the strong flavor of the mutton is objectionable, try to remove most of the fat from the meat, or parboil the meat before use. Add red wine for extra flavor.

4/e. Csángó Gulyás: Substitute 600 g (1¼ lb) of sauerkraut for the potatoes in Recipe 3. (If the sauerkraut is too sharp tasting, rinse it with cold water before use.) Instead of soup pasta *(csipetke)*, 60 g (⅓ cup) of rice is added to the soup. Just before serving add 2 dl (⅞ cup) sour cream to the soup and heat it briefly.

4/f. Kolozsvári Gulyás: Omit soup pasta *(csipetke)* from Recipe 3. Reduce potatoes to 600 g (1¼ lb), add cabbage cut in segments and substitute marjoram for the garlic.

4/g. Betyár Gulyás: Use smoked beef or smoked pork in this variation of Bográcsgulyás.

4/h. Likócsi Pork Gulyás Reduce the amount of lard (or shortening) used. Instead of beef, use pork. Replace the soup pasta with vermicelli. For the final flavoring use a small amount of lemon juice.

5.
Fisherman's Soup

This is a famous soup, which has just as many variations as *Gulyás soup.* It is a perennial favorite with tourists and Hungarians alike. The secret of good Fisherman's soup is in the preparation of the *Court Bouillon.* Use fresh carp heads, bones, skin, and fins. Boil the fish trimmings in 2 liters (2 qt) of water with onion, salt, a few green peppers (optional) and a tomato for 1–1½ hours. (This dish can also be prepared from smaller, less expensive fish.)

2 kg (4½ lb) carp   150 g (1 cup) green peppers
(live if possible)   70 g (1 medium) tomato
250 g (2 cups) onion, salt   30 g (2 lbs) paprika

Clean the fish and remove all entrails, making sure that the gall bladder is removed intact; it would make the soup inedible. Fillet the fish; even the skin may be removed. The edge of the thicker part of the fillet should be scored heavily. The fillet will be almost boneless if it is properly removed from the spine. Cut the fillets into two finger-thick slices, place them in a bowl with the roe and coral, salt and refrigerate. Prepare the *Court Bouillon* as described above. This can be done a day before the soup will be on the menu. When ready, strain it; the soup will be tastier if as many vegetables as possible are puréed and strained and then added to the soup. Heat the *Court Bouillon* to boiling point, then add the paprika. Ten minutes before serving, add the sliced fillet, the roe and coral.

A smooth, elegant Hungarian white wine goes best with the Fisherman's soup.

6.
Variations of the Fisherman's Soup

6/a. Fisherman's Soup à la Szeged: The preparation is similar to Recipe 5, but instead of just carp, four different kinds of fish are used. This results in a superior flavor. The usual ratio is 800 g (1¾ lb) carp, 500 g (1 lb) catfish, 350 g (¾ lb) sturgeon and 350 g (¾ lb) pike-perch.

6/b. Drinker's Fish Soup: This is also a variation of Recipe 5, but bay leaf is used in the *Court Bouillon,* and before serving, the soup is thickened. The thickening agent is 1 teaspoon of flour mixed in 2 dl (⅞ cup) sour cream and a small amount of lemon juice. The smooth sour cream mixture is stirred into the hot soup. Garnish with lemon rings.

6/c. Fisherman's Soup à la Kalocsa: The difference between this soup and Recipe 5 is that noodles are added to the soup. The noodle dough is prepared from 120 g (1 cup) flour, 1 egg and a pinch of salt. This will give a stiff dough. Roll it out and julienne finely. Dry the noodles in the oven without any addition of fat until golden yellow. Add the hot noodles to the hot soup just before the fish is completetly cooked.

6/d. Fisherman's Soup à la Paks: This regional dish is almost identical to the previous Recipe 6/c, except that the noodle dough is rolled more thinly and cut wider.

Soups

7.
Jókai Bean Soup

This flavorful soup is named after the popular and prolific writer Mór Jókai (1825–1904).

180 g (1 cup) kidney beans	300 g (½–¾ lb) smoked sausage
or 300 g (2 cups) fresh beans	40 g (3 Tbs) lard
300 g (½–¾ lb) smoked pig's hocks	30 g (6 Tbs) flour
100 g (¾ cup) carrots	30 g (¼ cup) onion
80 g (⅔ cup) white turnip	5 g (1 tsp) paprika, parsley
garlic, bay leaf	1.5 dl (⅔ cup) sour cream
150 g (1 cup) green pepper	30 g (¼ cup) flour
70 g (1 medium) fresh tomato	soup pasta (Recipe 14)

If kidney beans are used, wash them and soak them overnight. (Fresh shelled beans do not have to be soaked.) Cook the smoked pig's hocks (knuckle) in 1.5 liter (1½ qt) of water the day before cooking until tender. Skim the fat from the top of the water, heat the fat in a soup pot and slightly brown the sliced soup vegetable in it. When the vegetables start to brown, add the kidney beans with the water in which they were soaked, the cooking liquid of the pig's feet, a small amount of chopped garlic and a bay leaf, a green pepper cut into small pieces and a chopped tomato. Taste the mixture before you add any salt. While the beans are cooking, fry the smoked sausage and cut into slices. When the beans are cooked, prepare a roux with the sausage dripping and flour and flavor it with finely chopped onion. Finally, add the the paprika and chopped parsley. Pour the soup over the roux and bring to a boil again. Add the sour cream, soup pasta (csipetke) and fried sausage slices. Just before serving, cut the pig's hocks (knuckles) into small serving pieces and place them in a soup tureen, then add the soup. The soup can be further flavored with vinegar or tarragon vinegar; a small amount of sugar may be used to offset the sour taste of the vinegar.

I. Gulyás soup

Soups

8.
Ujházi's Chicken Soup

This soup honors the actor Ede Ujházi (1844–1915), who was a pioneer of the modern, realistic style of acting.

2 kg (4½ lb) chicken, hen or turkey	100 g (¾ cup) fresh green peas (shelled)
300 g (2⅓ cups) soup vegetables	100 g (1 cup) cauliflower
80 g (⅔ cup) celeriac	100 g (4 spears) asparagus
50 g (½ cup) kohlrabi	green pepper
40 g (⅓ cup) onion	For the noodles: 120 g (1 cup) flour
salt, black pepper, ginger	1 large egg (or 2 small), salt
60 g (1 cup) mushrooms	a bunch of parsley

Wash the poultry well and place it in a pot with 2 liters (2 qt) of cold water. When it starts to boil carefully remove the foam. Reduce heat and simmer for half an hour. Then add the soup vegetables, celeriac, kohlrabi, onions and spices. When the meat is cooked, remove it to a platter. Let the soup settle, then drain it carefully through cheese cloth or a fine sieve.

Meanwhile boil in salt water (preferably in separate pots) the small mushrooms (cut the mushrooms if large), green peas, cauliflower, asparagus and the diced green pepper. When the vegetables in the soup pot are cooked, remove them and julienne half of the carrots, celeriac and parsley. (Use the other half for another dish.)

Meanwhile, prepare the vermicelli. Mix the flour and eggs with a pinch of salt and just enough water to produce a stiff dough. Roll the dough very thinly, let it dry slightly, then cut it finely. Boil the noodles in salted water. Before serving time, add to the soup the cooked vegetables and the stock they were cooked in. Place the cut up meat in the soup tureen or plates. (A variation: julienne the skinless boneless meat.) Cover the meat with the cooked noodles, then add the boiling hot soup; at the last moment, sprinkle with finely chopped parsley.

In glass side dishes, serve prepared horseradish. Don't forget to place the pepper mill on the table.

II. Jókai bean soup

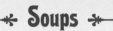

9.
Palóc Soup

This soup is the creation of János Gundel (the father of Károly Gundel) in honor of the famous Hungarian writer Kálmán Mikszáth (1847–1910) who was revered as the "great *Palóc*". (The Palóc are an ethnic group living in northern Hungary.)

400 g (¾–1 lb) mutton	250 g (1 ⅔ cups) fresh green beans
(preferably shoulder-blade)	2 dl (⅞ cup) sour cream
120 g (1 cup) onion	20 g (¼ cup) flour
60 g (¼ cup) lard	salt, garlic
10 g (2 tsp) paprika	caraway seeds
350 g (¾ lb) potatoes	bay leaf, dill

Cut the meat into 1 cm (½ in) cubes, and using the list of ingredients prepare a *pörkölt* as described in Recipe 39. While the *pörkölt* is cooking, cut the potatoes into small cubes, cut the green beans into strips about 2 cm (1 in) long. Cook both the potatoes and green beans, preferably in two separate pots, in salted water. When the meat is cooked, add to it the cooked potatoes and green beans with their cooking stock. This should give you about 2 liters (2 qt) of soup; if necessary, add more stock or water. Mix the flour with the sour cream and thicken the boiling soup with it. Finally, add a finely chopped sprig of dill. The soup can be made more piquant by the use of a small amount of lemon juice or tarragon vinegar.

10.
Pethes Soup
Named in honor of actor Imre Pethes (1864–1924).

1.1 kg (2½ lb) beef rump	60 g (½ cup) onion, garlic
1½ kg (3¼ lb) bones with marrow (shin)	30 g (2 Tbs) tomato paste
300 g (2⅓ cups) soup vegetables	salt, black pepper, ginger
80 g (¾ cup) celeriac	a bunch of chive
60 g (½ cup) kohlrabi	Vermicelli noodles
60 g (¾ cup) Savoy cabbage	(Recipe 6/c)

Boil the well-washed meat and shin-bones in 2 liters (2 qt) of water. Remove the gray foam which develops on the surface of the water, otherwise the soup will not be clear. Once it starts to boil, reduce heat and simmer the soup for an hour. After an hour, add the soup vegetables and spices. (Tomato paste or purée will impart a nice color to the soup.) When the meat is cooked, remove the bones and the meat to a platter. Let the soup settle, then carefully decant it.

Meanwhile cook the fine vermicelli in salted water according to Recipe 6/c.

At serving time place a slice of meat in the soup plate, two slices of bone marrow on the meat, next to it some cooked noodles and soup vegetables, then add the soup carefully and sprinkle it with chives. Toasted bread and prepared horseradish should accompany this soup.

For the further enjoyment of the bone marrow, black pepper, paprika and salt should be on hand for the guests.

11.
Consommé with Tokay Wine

600 g (1¼ lb/2½ cups) lean beef	60 g (½ cup) celeriac
1 egg white	25 g (3 Tbs) onion
20 g (4 tsp) tomato paste	30 g (½ cup) mushrooms
600 g (1¼ lb) beef bones	60 g (¾ cup) Savoy cabbage
300 g (2⅓ cups) soup vegetables	salt, pepper, ginger root, garlic

Grind the lean beef, mix it in a soup pot with the egg white and tomato paste, add 2 liters (2 qt) cold water or stock. Add the bones, sliced soup greens, spices. Bring it to a boil, then simmer for 3 hours. (You don't have to remove the foam as the soup boils.) Let the soup settle, then pour it through a cheese cloth very carefully. If the soup has a lot of fat on the surface, take it off with a spoon, then blot off the remaining fat with a paper napkin. Consommé can also be prepared from chicken or pheasant. Just before serving add the Tokay wine to the boiling soup, 3–5 cl (2–4 Tbs) per person. *Tokay Aszú* would give the most pronounced taste to this soup, but because it is sweet, we suggest the use of dry *Tokay Szamorodni*.

12.

Hungarian Green Bean Soup

300 g (¾ lb) bones	30 g (¼ cup) onion
100 g (¾ cup) carrots	30 g (¼ cup) flour
80 g (¾ cup) parsley root	2 g (dash) paprika
500 g (4½ cups) fresh green beans	parsley
20 g (2 Tbs) lard	1 dl (7 Tbs) sour cream
100 g (⅔ cup) green pepper	30 g (¼ cup) flour
50 g (1 small) tomato	vinegar, sugar
salt, garlic, black pepper	soup pasta (csipetke, Recipe 14)
20 g (2 Tbs) lard	

Prepare a stock from the bones and 2 liters (2 qt) of water. If the soup vegetables are not tender, cook them in the soup. The tender vegetables should be braised with the cut (2 cm, 1 in) green beans. Pour the soup over the braised vegetables, add diced green pepper, tomato, salt to taste, a clove of finely chopped garlic and black pepper. When all the vegetables are cooked, thicken the soup. Melt the lard (shortening), add the finely chopped onion, cook until transparent, add flour and lightly brown it, stir in the paprika quickly, add a small amount of cold water, then pour it into the soup. Add finely chopped parsley. Mix the flour and sour cream, stir into the soup, and bring to a boil. A few drops of vinegar and sugar may be added to the soup just before the soup pasta *(csipetke)* is added.

A similar method is used to prepare *potato soup Hungarian style:* use roux with paprika and soup pasta *(csipetke)* and sliced smoked sausage to make the soup even richer. If garlic is omitted, the same method will do for mushroom, asparagus or green pea soup, but for the last, substitute milk for the sour cream.

❧ Soups ❧

13.
Harvest Soup

This soup used to be prepared by the poor sharecroppers and farmers of the countryside.

1.4 kg (3 lb) fresh   *3 dl (1¼ cups) sour cream*
or smoked pork's feet, garlic   *80 g (¾ cup) flour*
salt, pepper   *1 egg, vinegar*

Cook the cleaned and split pig's feet with chopped garlic, salt and pepper, until tender. Remove the pig's feet from the cooking water, bone the meat and cut it into serving pieces. Mix the sour cream, egg and flour until you obtain a smooth paste, and add this to the soup. Flavor to taste with vinegar or tarragon, then add the meat to the hot soup. Smoked pig's feet improves the flavor, but be careful, it might be too salty.

14.
Soup Pasta
(Csipetke)

80 g (¾ cup) flour   *1 egg, salt*

Prepare a stiff dough from the flour and egg (do not use water). On a floured board roll it out as thinly as you can. Then with floured fingers pinch small fingernail size bits out of it. (The Hungarian name *csipetke* means pinched pieces.) Add the bits to the boiling soup; stir the soup a few times.
The pasta will be cooked when it comes to the surface of the soup, in about 2–3 minutes.

6.
Cold Appetizers

Cold party sandwiches as appetizers enjoy world-wide acceptance. The selection of sandwiches can be improved by the use of hard or other salamies, smoked sausage (kielbasa), prepared *gyulai* or *csabai* style, or boned pork loin roast stuffed with sausage, or goose liver (Recipe 23), and even ewe-cheese spread (Recipe 124). To decorate the sandwiches use green pepper, sprinkle with paprika or place a few small pieces of pimiento on top to achieve a very appetizing appearance.

15.
Jellied Fisherman's Broth

Produce a *Court Bouillon* according to Recipe 5, make it very rich with the addition of small fish, strain the soup but do not purée the vegetables and fish.

At the end, while the fish fillet is cooking, poach a few small tomatoes in the soup for half a minute, poach a few green pepper rings for 2 minutes. (For the poaching use a large slotted spoon or soup strainer which can be immersed easily in the soup and removed without scalding yourself.) When the fillet and roe are cooked, arrange them nicely in a glass or ceramic dish or individual serving dishes, decorate with slices of hard-boiled egg, poached green pepper rings, peeled poached tomato segments.

While the decorated fish platters are cooling, place a small amount of skimmed soup in the refrigerator; if it jells, it can be used as it is. If it won't jell, add a small amount of gelatin to the soup. If gelatin is used, clarify the soup. Mix 2 egg whites with half a teaspoon of tomato paste and a small amount of water and whip until foamy. Slowly add the soup to this mixture, then heat it to boiling point. Let it stand for 5–10 minutes to settle before straining it through a cheese cloth.

Before the soup jells, spoon it over the pre-arranged fish and refrigerate.

16.
Pike-Perch Slices à la Tihany

1.8 kg (4 lb) pike-perch or	For the mixed vegetable (French) salad:
900 g (2 lb) pike-perch fillet	250 g (2 cups) carrots
salt	200 g (½ lb) potatoes
black pepper	150 g (1 cup) green peas (canned)
———	100 g (1 cup) apples
For the mayonnaise:	100 g (⅔ cup) diced gherkins
3 egg yolks	mayonnaise (as in Recipe 16)
juice of 1 lemon	salt, pepper, lemon juice, mustard
salt, cayenne pepper	———
5 dl (1 pt) oil	3 hard-boiled eggs
———	lettuce leaves
10 g (2 tsp) gelatin	300 g (1¼ cups) fish aspic
30 g (1 oz) smoked salmon (lox)	4 dl (1¾ cups) tartar sauce
tarragon leaves	or green sauce or Csíki sauce
	(Recipe 102)

Fillet the fish and remove the skin. Use the bones, skin, fish heads, fins and 3–4 dl (1¼–1¾ cups) water to make a *Court Bouillon*. While the soup is cooking remove any remaining bones from the fillets and cut into 12 triangular pieces, each roughly the same size. Small pieces of fish outside the triangle could be folded under and lightly pounded into the triangle, or cut those small fish pieces off. Lightly salt and pepper the fillets, cook them slowly in the Court Bouillon. Let the fish cool down in the soup.

To prepare the mayonnaise: place the egg yolks in a ceramic or glass mixing bowl, add salt, a few drops of vinegar, a small amount of lemon juice. Using a wire whisk, beat the egg yolks while slowly but steadily adding the oil to the mixture. The sauce should thicken as you proceed. If the product is too thick, add a few drops of lemon juice and then continue with the oil.

Divide the mayonnaise into two bowls. One half is mixed with gelatin dissolved in lukewarm *Court Buillon*. The other half is used in the mixed vegetable salad.

To prepare the mixed vegetable salad: peel and cube the carrots (1 cm cubes, ½ in). Cook the carrots in salted water, drain them and let them cool. Boil the potatoes unpeeled. When cooked, peel and

cube the potatoes too. Peel and cube the apples. Drain the canned green peas. In a large bowl mix all the cooled, cubed ingredients, add the salt, pepper, mustard and lemon juice to taste, then mix in half the mayonnaise. Spread the mixed salad evenly over a serving platter. Remove the fish fillets from the *Court Bouillon* and let them drain. Coat the drained fish triangles with the mayonnaise-gelatin mixture. (If the coating mixture is too thick, thin it with melted aspic. If it is too thin and dripping off the fish, add a small amount of gelatin.) When the coating mixture is set, decorate the fish slices with the smoked salmon (lox) and tarragon leaves.

At serving time place the decorated fish slices on the prepared mixed-salad platter. Further decorate the platter with cubed aspic, lettuce leaves and hard-boiled egg wedges. Serve tartar, green or *Csíki* sauce (Recipe 102) in a separate small bowl.

17.
Fish Salad Szeged Style

For the sauce:
30 g (Tbs) finely chopped onions
½ bunch finely chopped chives
salt, vinegar, pepper
1 dl (7 Tbs) oil
5 g (1 tsp) paprika
80 g (6 Tbs) red pepper paste

For the fish salad:
700 g (1½ lb/5 cups) cooked fish
200 g (1⅓ cups) green pepper
100 g (1 small) tomato
2 hard-boiled eggs
lettuce leaves

First prepare the piquant sauce; this will allow time for the flavors to blend. Then remove all bones from the cooked fish, flake the fish and chill it. Dice the green pepper, cook in the cooking water of the fish for 2–3 minutes. Scald the tomatoes, pull off the skin, remove the seeds and slice. In a bowl, combine the fish, tomatoes, green pepper; add the piquant sauce and small amount of lemon juice to taste. Chill for a few hours. Before serving, decorate the fish salad with lettuce leaves and slices of hard-boiled eggs.

III. Serbian carp

18.
City Park Salad

One of the favorite summer dishes of the guests of the Gundel restaurant located at the City Park in Budapest.

300 g (¾ lb) kidney potatoes	*1 roast chicken*
3 eggs	*salt, lemon juice*
2 small tart apples	*Worcestershire sauce*
200 g (2 cups) cucumbers	*mustard, chives, pepper*
300 g (3 small) tomatoes	*mayonnaise (Recipe 16)*
30 small crayfish	*prepared from 2 egg yolks*
1 head of Boston lettuce	*3.5 dl (1½ cups) oil*

Boil the potatoes without peeling them. Hard-boil the eggs. Peel and core the apples. Peel the cucumbers and tomatoes. Cook the crayfish, remove the meat from the crayfish. Chop the potatoes and apples into very thin pieces and place them in a mixing bowl. Slice the cucumbers very thin; also slice the tomatoes and eggs and add them to the bowl. Cut the lettuce leaves into strips, as wide as your finger. The white meat of the chicken should be sliced into thin slices, and the dark meat julienned very thinly. Save a few slices of egg, tomatoes and chicken breast together with crayfish for decorating the salad. Mix the contents of the bowl carefully, and add the spices. The mayonnaise should be added at the last minute, otherwise the tomato and cucumber juice will make it watery. Place lettuce leaves on a glass platter. Pile the salad on it, and decorate with the reserved slices of meat, crayfish tails, tomatoes and eggs.

IV. Poached eggs Bakony style

19.
Tomato Stuffed with Fish

1 kg (2¼ lb) tomatoes   *Mayonnaise (Recipe 16)*
vinegar, oil, salt, pepper   *Mixed vegetable salad (Recipe 16)*
parsley, sugar   *180 g (¾ cup) aspic*
500 g (1–1¼ lb) cooked fish

The day before you want to serve the stuffed tomato, scald 1 large or, preferably, 2 small ripe tomatoes per person and pull the skin off. Cut the top off (about ⅓ of the tomato), carefully remove the seeds and pulp. In a deep bowl mix a marinade made out of vinegar, oil, salt, pepper, parsley and a small amount of sugar. Marinate the tomatoes, including the cut off tops for 24 hours. Let the tomato bottoms drain after this time. Cube the fish which was poached in salted and slightly vinegary water. Divide the mayonnaise into three parts. Mix the fish with ⅓ of the mayonnaise and stuff the tomatoes with the mixture. Coat the tomatoes with the next third of the mayonnaise. The last third is used in the preparation of the mixed vegetable salad. Sprinkle the finely chopped parsley on the tomatoes; replace the tops. Spread the mixed vegetable salad on a glass platter, placing the tomatoes on top of the mixed vegetable salad base. Decorate the platter with lettuce leaves and aspic before serving it.

The tomatoes can be stuffed with a meat salad instead of fish, in which case use finely chopped Hungarian ham, or else *fish salad Szeged style* (Recipe 17). However, if you use fish salad, do not coat the tomatoes with mayonnaise; sprinkle chopped hard-boiled eggs on the stuffed tomatoes instead.

20.
Eggs in Aspic Munkácsy Style

This tasty dish was named after the world famous Hungarian painter Mihály Munkácsy (1844–1900).

For the fish salad:	*sauce remoulade (see below)*
250 g (9 oz) cooked fish	————
200 g (2 small) tomatoes	*12 poached eggs*
120 g (1¼ cups) mushrooms	*tarragon*
200 g (1½ cups) celeriac	*600 g (2½ cups) fish aspic*

Cook and cube the peeled tomatoes, mushrooms and celeriac. Flake the cooked fish. Mix the vegetables and fish with a small amount of melted aspic and *sauce remoulade*. Spread the fish salad on a round glass platter.

To prepare the sauce remoulade: using an egg yolk and 1.75 dl (¾ cup) oil prepare mayonnaise as in Recipe 16. Add to the mayonnaise: sweet cream, mustard, salt, black pepper, sugar, capers, anchovy paste, chives, tarragon leaves and finely chopped gherkins. This will result in a piquant sauce. Chill the remoulade well.

Poach the eggs in salted water to which vinegar is added for 3 minutes. The yolk of the eggs should remain soft. Lift out the poached eggs carefully and trim the edges. Pour aspic into the bottom of 12 small molds. Let the aspic set in the mold, then decorate each with tarragon leaves, place a poached egg on the top of the set aspic, fill the mold with lukewarm aspic and refrigerate the molds. Before serving, unmold the eggs on the top of the fish salad platter by dipping the mold into hot water for a short time. Decorate with aspic and lettuce leaves.

Cold Appetizers

21.
Stuffed Dill Gherkins

600 g (1¼ lb) mushrooms	lemon juice
½ dl (4 Tbs) oil	900 g (2 lb) dill gherkins (Recipe 96)
30 g (3 Tbs) onion	250 g (3 small) tomatoes
salt, black pepper	200 g (1 cup) mixed vegetables salad
mayonnaise (Recipe 16) prepared from	(Recipe 16)
2 egg yolks and 3.5 dl (1½ cups) oil	2 hard-boiled eggs
Worcestershire sauce	lettuce leaves, aspic

Chop the well-washed mushrooms and drain thoroughly. Sauté the chopped onion in the oil. Add the chopped mushrooms to the sautéd onion, add the black pepper, salt, cook the mushrooms until all the liquid is evaporated, then cool. When the mushrooms are cooled, add just enough mayonnaise to obtain a spread. Flavor the mayonnaise mushroom spread with Worcestershire sauce and lemon juice, then chill. Peel the chilled, dill gherkins and tomato. Cut the peeled gherkins lengthwise and remove most of the seeds. Fill one side of the split gherkins with the mushroom spread and replace the top part.
For serving, spread the mixed vegetable salad on the platter, top it with the stuffed gherkins, then cover the gherkins with mayonnaise. Place 3 thin slices of tomatoes on top of each gherkin. Decorate the platter with parsley, lettuce leaves, chopped egg and aspic.

22.
Jellied Pork

2 kg (4½ lb) young pork	80 g (⅔ cup) carrots
salt, peppercorns	50 g (⅓–½ cup) turnip
garlic, bay leaf	30 g (¼ cup) celeriac
3 g (½ tsp) paprika	50 g (½ cup) green pepper (in strips)
150 g (1 large) onion	1 hard-boiled egg

Wash the meat very well. If necessary, scald it with boiling water to remove the skin. Place the meat in a large pot with 3 liters (3 qt) of cold water and all the other ingredients except the egg and simmer slowly until the meat is tender. Remove the meat from the cooking stock and bone it. Cut the meat in small serving pieces and arrange in a large glass or ceramic casserole or individual serving dishes. Decorate the meat with slices of hard-boiled eggs and cooked vegetable sliced with a corrugated knife. The drained stock is handled like the stock in Recipe 15: test, remove fat, clarify. When the stock has cooled but not yet set, spoon it over the arranged meat. Jellied meat can also be prepared by using pig's head, feet, tails and skin. To enhance the flavor, cook some smoked meat with the pig trimmings. Serve the jellied meat with vinegar, lemon juice, prepared horseradish, or chopped pickles. Paprika and black pepper should accompany the dish.

23.
Goose Liver in Goose Fat

1 kg (2¼ lb) goose liver	1 dl (7 Tbs) white wine
150 g (¾ cup) goose fat	5 g (1 tsp) paprika
or lard, salt, peppercorns	1–2 green peppers
80 g (1 medium) onion	and tomatoes

Soak the liver in milk for an hour. Heat up the goose fat or lard and brown the salted liver, then add the peppercorns and sliced onion. When the onion starts to brown, add a small amount of wine and water. Cover the pan, lower the heat, and simmer the liver. If necessary, add more wine and water. When the liver is cooked through, remove the cover and place the dish into the preheated oven (medium hot). While baking the liver, turn and baste often, until all sides are pink-colored, but do not dry it out. Place the liver on a plate and refrigerate until well chilled. Slice the liver with a sharp knife dipped in hot water to facilitate slicing. Use the fried onion rings as decoration on the slices of liver. Heat up the dripping, add the paprika, and strain it on top of the liver. Chill again. Decorate the edge of the platter with slices of tomatoes and green pepper. Serve with baked potatoes.

Some people like to prepare the liver with garlic. However, it is more practical to serve toast and peeled garlic cloves with the liver, so people who like the taste of garlic can rub their toast with the garlic cloves. The left-over dripping makes a tasty base for sandwiches.

7.
Hot Appetizers

Most of our hot appetizer recipes are for fish or crayfish. Some people will consider a fish dish to be an integral part of the menu. A hot fish dish after a cold soup is a welcome sight. Even after a cold appetizer consisting of egg or mushroom for example, a hot fish dish will be well received. Make sure you balance the hot and cold appetizers. If one is a fairly substantial fare, the other should be lighter. If one is in a sauce, the other should be without sauce.

24.
Serbian Carp

1.5 kg (3¼ lb) potatoes	50 g (¼ cup) lard
400 g (¾ lb) green pepper	200 g (2 cups) thinly sliced onion
200 g (2 medium) tomatoes	
———	———
	80 g (6 Tbs) lard
1.2 kg (2½–2¾ lb) boneless–skinless carp	———
150 g (6 slices–1 package) smoked bacon	30 g (¼ cup) flour
salt	3 g (½ tsp) paprika
15 g (1 Tbs) paprika	4 dl (1½ cups) sour cream
———	150 g (6 slices–1 pkg) smoked bacon
	parsley

Parboil the potatoes, peel and slice them. Core the green peppers, slice them and the peeled tomatoes into nice rounds.

Cut 3–4 cm (1½ in) slits in the fish fillet, and stick pieces of bacon in the slits (i.e. lard the fish). Sprinkle salt and paprika on the fillets. Grease a deep rectangular baking dish or casserole. Place the potato slices in it. On the top of the potatoes place the fish slices; if you have fish roe, use that, too. Cover the fish with thinly sliced onion rings, green pepper and tomato slices. Sprinkle the melted lard all over the casserole. Bake in a medium hot oven until the fish is half-cooked. Mix the sour

cream with the flour and paprika and pour it over the fish casserole. Bake until the top is light brown.

Just before serving, sprinkle more sour cream over the dish and decorate with bacon slices, which were slit before frying into the shape of a cockscomb, and sprinkle with finely chopped parsley.

25.
Trout Stuffed with Goose Liver

60 g (¾ lb) goose liver	2 hard rolls
salt, black pepper	5 cl (3½ Tbs) wine
5 cl (3½ Tbs) cognac	5 cl (3½ Tbs) sweet cream
———	2 eggs
2 kg (4½ lb) trout	salt, parsley
1 dl (7 Tbs) vinegar	120 g (½ cup) butter

The day before you want to serve this dish, cut the liver into small cubes, season it with salt and pepper, then marinate in cognac.

Pick 6 trout about the same size and clean them, but keep the heads on. Wash the trout in vinegar-water. Cut the rolls into small cubes, soak the cubes in a wine and sweet cream mixture. Add the eggs, chopped parsley and salt to the rolls and combine until you get a smooth stuffing. Add the cubed marinated liver to the stuffing. Salt the fish and stuff them. Butter aluminum foil or wax paper and roll each fish into an individual packet. Bake the packets for 20 min. in a slow oven. Remove the fish from the foil, arrange them on a platter, pour melted butter over them and serve with parsleyed potatoes. The fish can be accompanied by mayonnaise, tartar sauce or *Csíki* sauce (Recipe 102).

26.
Fillets of Young Pike-Perch Hungarian Style

2 kg (4½ lb) pike-perch for fillets	3 dl (1¼ cups) sour cream
80 g (6 Tbs) lard	1 dl (7 Tbs) white wine
150 g (⅞ cup) chopped onion	20 g (1 Tbs) butter
150 g (1 cup) chopped green pepper	30 g (2 Tbs) lard
60 g (1 small) tomato	30 g (¼ cup) flour
15 g (1 Tbs) paprika	salt

Clean and fillet the fish. Remove the skin and salt the fillets. Brown the onion in the lard. Cook the fish head, bones, skin with the browned onion, chopped green pepper and tomatoes in ½ liter (1 pt) of water for ½–1 hours. Drain the cooking liquid and add the sour cream to it. Meanwhile, the fish should be steamed in a small amount of wine, covered with greased wax paper. Thicken the sour cream and fish stock mixture with roux prepared from the lard and flour. Arrange the cooked fish in a glass dish and strain the sauce over it. Serve with buttered parsleyed potatoes or with galushka dumplings (Recipe 91).

27.
Fillets of Young Pike-Perch Peasant Style

Omit the sour cream from Recipe 26. Cut 150 g (6 slices) bacon into small cubes, and render the fat from them. Reserve the fried bacon bits and add them to the gravy just before serving. Fry the onion in the bacon fat and a small amount of lard for a smoky flavor.

28.
Giant Pike-Perch (Fogas)
or Pike-Perch with Crayfish Pörkölt

The dish is one of the most successful creations of Károly Gundel. It combines French and Hungarian cuisine to produce an offspring which is delectable to the taste and satisfying to the eye.

2 kg (4½ lb) giant pike-perch	*For the Hollandaise sauce:*
or pike-perch	7 egg yolks
or 1 kg (2¼ lb) pike-perch fillet, salt	1.5 dl (⅔ cup) heavy cream
40 g (3 Tbs) butter	250 g (1 cup) butter
2 dl (⅞ cup) white wine	salt
————	lemon juice
4 portions crayfish pörkölt	cayenne pepper
(Recipe 32)	

Fillet the fish. Prepare a stock from the salted fish bones and skin. Butter a baking dish, place the salted fillets in it, pour wine over the fish and stew, covered with buttered wax paper, in a slow oven.

Prepare the crayfish *pörkölt* according to Recipe 32. Reduce the number of crayfish to 40; use the stock which you prepared from the fish bones.

Just before serving make the *Hollandaise sauce*. Place the egg yolks and cream in the top of the double boiler, over simmering water. Beat the mixture constantly with a wire whisk until foamy. Remove from the stove, and continuing to whisk add the melted butter very slowly. Flavor with lemon juice and cayenne pepper to taste. The Hollandaise sauce should be velvety smooth and of whipped cream consistency. Drain the fish fillets thoroughly, place them on a preheated plate, and pour the Hollandaise sauce over the fish. Arrange the crayfish *pörkölt* in strips over the fish. Serve with parsleyed potatoes.

29.
Giant Pike-Perch or Pike-Perch Gundel Style

This is also a Károly Gundel creation. Its taste surpasses all expectations.

1 kg (2¼ lb) leaf spinach	For the Mornay sauce:
20 g (1 Tbs) butter	40 g (3 Tbs) butter
salt, black pepper	30 g (¼ cup) flour
——————	3 dl (1¼ cups) milk
150 g (2¼ cups) mushrooms	1 dl (7 Tbs) heavy cream
30 g (2 Tbs) butter	3 egg yolks
salt, pepper, parsley	50 g (½ cup) grated cheese
——————	salt, nutmeg
800 g (1¾ lb) boneless pike	——————
60 g (½ cup) flour	30 g (¼ cup) grated cheese
1 egg, 3 egg whites (use the yolk	20 g (1 Tbs) butter
for the Mornay sauce)	500 g (1 lb) potatoes
120 g (3 cups) breadcrumbs	2 egg yolks
150 g (⅔ cup) lard or butter	

Cook the spinach in salted water with a pinch of bicarbonate of soda (for color retention). Drain and rinse with cold water, squeeze well, flavor with butter and black pepper.

Braise the finely sliced mushrooms in butter with salt, black pepper and finely chopped parsley until the liquid has evaporated.

Cut the fish into six portions. Salt lightly. Dip the fish slices into flour, then eggs, then breadcrumbs, and fry in hot lard.

Spread the spinach on a large platter and place the fish slices on top of the spinach. Portion out the mushrooms on the fish slices, then cover with the *Mornay sauce,* which is prepared like a Bechamel sauce (see Recipe 56), but using the ingredients listed above. Finally, sprinkle the platter with grated cheese and melted butter, and brown the top in a hot oven.

The edge of the platter could be decorated with mashed potato piped using a pastry bag *(Pommes Duchesse)*. To make the mashed potatoes trim, cook and mash the potatoes. Add 20 g (1 Tbs) butter, salt and 2 egg yolks and whip until fluffy and smooth. Flavor the mashed potatoes with nutmeg. (Originally, this dish was served without mushrooms.)

30.
Sterlet Carpathian Style
(with dill-flavored crayfish ragout)

30 crayfish	100 g (7 Tbs) butter
1.8 kg (4 lb) sterlet	200 g (3 cups) mushrooms
or sturgeon (one large	salt, black pepper, parsley
or 6 x 300 g (6 x 10 oz. pieces)	———
bunch of dill	40 g (6 Tbs) flour
———	¼ l (1 cup) heavy cream
1 dl (7 Tbs) white wine	

Cook the crayfish and prepare the crayfish butter according to Recipe 32. Clean the fish, leaving the head on, dip in boiling water, rinse in cold water, remove the skin with a sharp knife, and pull out the rubbery muscle which is next to the spine. (Winding the muscle on a two-pronged fork facilitates its removal.) Season the fish with salt.

Chop the dill finely and slice the mushrooms thinly.

Place the fish in a baking pan, pour small amount of fish stock or wine under it. Cover the pan with greased wax paper and stew the fish in moderate oven until it is done. While the fish is stewing, brown the mushrooms in the butter, add the salt, black pepper, chopped parsley. Add the dill. (The flavor of the dill should be predominant.) Cook a while longer, under a lid, then add some fish stock. Mix the flour and cream until smooth and stir into the mushrooms. Add the crayfish meat and butter to the mushrooms. Bring to a boil again, pour the mixture on top of the fish. Simmer, shaking once in a while, until the fish is tender. Serve with rice or buttered potatoes.

This dish can also be prepared from perch or pike.

31.
Catfish in Sauerkraut

1.2 kg (1½–1¾ lb) boneless catfish	20 g (1 Tbs) lard
1.2 kg (5 cups) sauerkraut	50 g (6 Tbs) flour
120 g (4 slices) smoked bacon	½ bunch of dill
80 g (½ cup) finely chopped onion	3 dl (1¼ cups) sour cream
30 g (2 Tbs) lard	————
160 g (2 cups) green pepper	½ dl (3 Tbs) sour cream
80 g (1 small) tomato	2 g (dash) paprika
20 g (1 Tbs) paprika	10 g (2 tsp) lard
black pepper	

Remove all the skin from the fish. Be careful with the use of salt, adjust it to the saltiness of the sauerkraut. The sauerkraut should be rinsed to remove some of the salt and sour taste.
Cut the smoked bacon into small squares, fry it until translucent, add the finely chopped onion, a small amount of lard, peeled and chopped tomatoes, green pepper rings and paprika. Stir the mixture, then immediately add the sauerkraut and black pepper. Simmer for about an hour. Meanwhile, prepare a light roux with chopped dill and thicken the cooled sauerkraut with it. Add the fish (sliced) and simmer under a lid in a medium hot oven for 20 minutes. Add the sour cream and boil the sauerkraut again.
In the serving dish place the sauerkraut below and the fish slices on top. Pour a small amount of sour cream and hot lard with paprika on top of the dish.

32.
Crayfish Pörkölt

50 crayfish (small)	1.5 dl (⅔ cup) consommé
salt, caraway seed, parsley	(can be made from bouillon cubes)
80 g (6 Tbs) butter	————
(for crayfish butter)	80 g (6 Tbs) butter
6 g (1 tsp) paprika	15 g (2 Tbs) flour

Cook the well-washed live crayfish in slightly salty water with some caraway seeds and parsley. Remove the meat from the cooked crayfish tails and claws; discard the intestines. Crush the remains of the crayfish in a mortar and pestle. Heat the butter in a pan, brown the crushed crayfish until all the liquid has evaporated.

To make crayfish butter, add stock to the pan to cover the fried crayfish bits and boil for 20 minutes, Drain through a sieve or cheese cloth. Let this stock cool, then remove all the fat which comes to the surface. This "fat" is called *crayfish butter.* Reboil the crayfish butter to evaporate any water which it may contain. (By the way, left-over crayfish butter will last in the refrigerator for a few weeks and makes a wonderful flavoring agent.)

Heat the crayfish meat in the crayfish butter, add paprika and about 1.5 dl (⅔ cup) of the crayfish stock or consommé. Mix the butter with flour and dribble it on top of the stew. Do not boil it any more. Shake the pot as the stew starts to thicken. Check to see if additional flavoring is required. Serve the crayfish *pörkölt* with steamed rice, place in a separate bowl.

Instead of crayfish, shrimp or crab can also be used to prepare this dish.

33.
Crayfish Strudel

40 crayfish (small)	1.5 dl (⅔ cup) sour cream
160 g (¾ cup) butter	20 g (1 Tbs) butter

2 hard crescent rolls	Use the crayfish butter as follows:
½ dl (3 Tbs) heavy cream	½ for the stuffing
1 egg, 2 egg yolks	⅓ for the strudel leaves
salt, mace	⅕ on top of the stuffed strudel

Follow Recipe 32 for the preparation of the *crayfish* and *crayfish butter,* with the exception of the quantity of butter, which should be increased to 160 g (¾ cup) because you'll need more crayfish butter.

Soak the hard crescent rolls in the heavy cream. When softened, squeeze them out and chop the rolls and combine them with the chopped crayfish meat. In a mixing bowl whip an egg, 2 egg yolks, the salt and mace, the sour cream and 80 g (6 Tbs) crayfish butter until light and foamy.

Hot Appetizers

Prepare the strudel dough according to Recipe 115. Stretch it out very thinly, sprinkle the dough with melted crayfish butter, spread the crayfish stuffing on it and roll the strudel up loosely. Place the strudel on a buttered cookie sheet, spread melted crayfish butter over it, then bake in a medium hot oven until rosy brown. (Crayfish sauce may be served with the strudel in a separate bowl.) Instead of crayfish, shrimp or crab can also be used to prepare this dish.

34.
Scrambled Eggs Santelli

The Italian fencing master Italo Santelli (1866–1945) lived in Hungary for a long time. He used to order this dish for breakfast at the Hotel Gellért.

300 g (½–¾ lb) smoked sausage (Debreceni)   *40 g (3 Tbs) lard*
120 (1 medium) tomato   *12 eggs, salt, black pepper*
240 g (½ lb) green pepper   *120 g (1 cup) grated cheese*
120 g (4 slices) smoked bacon

Peel the sausage and tomatoes and core the green pepper. Cut all three into rounds. Cut the bacon without its rind into small squares and fry it lightly in lard. Then lightly fry the sausage in the fat and bacon and add the green peppers. When the peppers start to soften, add the tomato. Fry the mixture until the liquid has evaporated. In a bowl lightly mix the eggs, then add them to the frying pan. Add salt and pepper to taste and finish frying. Sprinkle grated cheese on top of the eggs before serving.

35.
Poached Eggs Hadik Style

This dish honors the memory of Count András Hadik (1710–1790). He was Marshall, Supreme Commander, and writer of war history books.

10 g (1 Tbs) butter	50 g (¼ cup) butter
30 g (½ cup) parsley (finely chopped)	50 g (½ cup) flour
1 hard roll	3 dl (1¼ cups) milk
400 g (1¾ cups) chopped veal	2 dl (⅞ cup) heavy cream
1 egg	———
salt, pepper	1 egg yolk
———	1.5 dl (⅔ cup) heavy cream
60 g (7 Tbs) chopped onion	20 g (2 Tbs) butter
20 g (1 Tbs) lard	20 g (7 Tbs) breadcrumbs
300 g (1¼ cups) mushrooms	60 g (¼ cup) lard
salt, pepper, parsley	12 poached eggs

Melt the butter in a frying pan; sauté the chopped parsley in the butter. In a small bowl soak the roll in water, then squeeze dry. In a large bowl mix the chopped veal, one egg, the roll, sautéd parsley, salt and pepper. Divide the mixture into 12 parts and form 12 flat patties.

In the frying pan melt the lard, sauté the chopped onion, add the finely cut mushrooms, salt, pepper and parsley to the onion, and fry it lightly.

Meanwhile, prepare a light roux from the butter and flour, add the cold milk and cream, then the mushroom mixture. Bring the mushroom gravy to full boil. Lower the heat. Mix the egg yolk with the 1½ dl (⅔ cup) of cream, and immediately stir this mixture into the gravy. Continue stirring until smooth. Finally, dot small pieces of butter on top of the gravy.

Roll the veal patties in the breadcrumbs and fry them in lard.

Poach the eggs in salted, vinegary water, for 3 minutes. Rinse the eggs and trim the edges. Place an egg on each veal patty; spoon the mushroom sauce over the eggs. Sprinkle chopped parsley over the gravy, and serve immediately. (Rice as a side dish goes nicely with this meal.)

36.
Poached Eggs Bakony Style

Bakony is a mountainous area located north of Lake Balaton. The *Bakony* mushroom sauce can be used not only over poached eggs, but it is delicious over fish or veal also. The meat should be partially cooked first, then added to the sauce to complete the cooking. (Serve the meat with buttered potatoes, galushka, see Recipe 91, or rice.) If the mushroom is chopped extremely finely, when it is soft you can push it through a sieve and add consommé or bouillon soup to it to obtain a very tasty mushroom cream soup.

100 g (⅔ cup) finely chopped onion	160 g (1 cup) cubed green pepper
120 g (½ cup) butter	80 g (1 small) tomato
15 g (1 Tbs) paprika	3 dl (1¼ cups) sour cream
350 g (5 cups) mushrooms	30 g (¼ cup) flour
salt, garlic	12 poached eggs
ground caraway seeds, parsley	4 portions of steamed rice

Sauté the finely chopped onion in the butter. Sprinkle the paprika on the onion; stir it in quickly. Add the sliced mushrooms immediately to the onions, then add the salt, a small amount of chopped garlic, pulverized caraway seeds and chopped parsley. When all the water has been evaporated, add the cubed green peppers and tomatoes to the mushrooms. Cook with the addition of a small amount of water, covered, until all the vegetables are done. Mix the sour cream and flour. When the vegetables are cooked, thicken the sauce by adding the sour cream and flour mixture.

Poach the eggs for 3 minutes in salted water, adding a few drops of vinegar. Rinse and trim the poached eggs. Place the eggs on the steamed rice. Pour the mushroom sauce over the rice and eggs. Sprinkle chopped parsley over the sauce. You can also pour a small amount of lard with paprika over the mushroom sauce; or even better, which is more to the Hungarian taste, make the sauce with fried smoked bacon.

V. Veal paprikás
VI. Gundel tokány

37.
Pancakes Hortobágy

12 savory pancakes   20 g (¼ cup) flour
750 g (3¼ cups) veal pörkölt   4 dl (1¾ cups) sour cream
½ dl (¼ cup) sour cream

Prepare the pancakes (crepes) according to Recipe 108, but instead of sugar, add some salt. Prepare the veal *pörkölt* according to Recipe 39, reducing the quantity of meat to 750 g (3¼ cups). When the meat is tender, remove it from the sauce and chop it up finely. Add one third of the sauce to the chopped meat and add the sour cream; cook this until the consistency is pasty. Divide this paste and place it on each pancake, fold two edges over the filling, then roll up. Mix the flour and sour cream into the sauce and bring it to a boil. Strain the sauce over the filled pancakes. (If necessary, reheat the pancakes in the oven before adding the sauce.) Instead of veal, chicken *pörkölt* can also be used for filling these pancakes or crepes, called *palacsinta* in Hungarian.

38.
Hungarian Macaroni

80 g (3 slices) smoked bacon   salt, garlic
50 g (¼ cup) lard   140 g (1 cup) diced green pepper
150 g (¾ cup) onion   60 g (1 small) tomato
15 g (1 Tbs) paprika   600 g (5 cups) macaroni
500 g (3½ cups) veal   120 g (1 cup) grated cheese

Fry the bacon until it is translucent, add the chopped onion and fry it until it is light brown. Add the paprika, then immediately add the meat which is cut approximately pea size. Add salt and a small amount of garlic; if it loses its liquid, add a small amount of water.
When the meat is almost done, add the green peppers and tomato cut into smal cubes. Simmer until almost all of the liquid is used up.
Cook the macaroni and add to the meat. Place the mixture in an oven-proof dish and sprinkle with cheese. Heat in the oven for a few minutes.

8.
Meat Dishes

Now we shall discuss the main course. The choices, both in the method of preparation and in the variety of raw materials, are greatly increased.

The sequence will start with *pörkölt, paprikás* and *tokány*. These are varieties of stews. Then we will proceed to dishes containing sauerkraut, continuing with beef, veal and pork entrées, and finally, we shall give recipes for poultry and game.

39.
Pörkölt

This typical product of the Hungarian kitchen is similar to the French *ragout*. The most often used cuts are the juicy neck, breast, blade or hocks, but other slightly bony cuts may also be used.

A *pörkölt's* sauce is not thickened. It should be flavorful and just barely cover the meat.

The preparation of the different types of *pörkölts* is very similar, but the ratio of ingredients varies somewhat; also the flavoring agents vary.

The *chart* below will help to summarize the main ingredients of the different types of *pörkölts*. (Round off the ounces according to your discretion!) The boneless meat should be cut into 2–3 cm (approx. 1 in) cubes. If the meat is on the bone, each piece should weigh about 40–50 g (1½–2 oz). Cut a chicken into 8–10 pieces.

Onion should be just wilted in lard for beef, mutton or game *pörkölt*. For any other type of *pörkölt*, fry the onions to a light yellow color. Reduce the heat, add the paprika, stir it rapidly, then add the meat and salt, browning the meat while stirring it. When the meat is well browned, add a small amount of water or stock, spices and herbs. Cover the pot and simmer the *pörkölt*. Stir occasionally. If necessary, add more liquid, but very sparingly. Do not boil the meat; it should be almost fried. When the meat begins to soften, add the green pepper and tomatoes cut into cubes, and simmer until the meat is tender. Serve with small galushka dumplings (Recipe 91), or with noodles or *tarhonya* (Recipe 90), or with boiled potatoes. Make sure that some piquant pickles are also served with this dish.

	Boneless meat or With bones (kg)	Lard (g)	Onion (g)	Paprika (g)	Salt	Garlic	Caraway seeds	Marjoram	Wine	Green pepper (g)	Tomatoes (fresh) (g)
Veal, lamb	1–1,25	120	250	20	+	?	–	–	–	200	100
	35–44 oz.	4.2 oz	8.8 oz.	0.7 oz.							
Beef, mutton, deer, rabbit	1–1,5	120	250	20	+	+	+	?	?	200	100
	35–53 oz.	4.2 oz.	8.8 oz.	0.7 oz.						7 oz.	3.5 oz.
Pork, pig, boar	1–1,500	80	250	20	+	+	+	–	–	160	80
	35–53 oz.	2.8 oz.	8.8 oz.	0.7 oz.						5.6 oz.	2.8 oz.
Chicken	2	120	180	20	+	–	?	–	–	200	100
	70 oz.	4.2 oz.	6.3 oz.	0.7 oz.						7 oz.	3.5 oz.
Goose, duck, turkey	3	80	180	20	+	+	–	–	–	200	100
	105 oz.	2.8 oz.	6.3 oz	0.7 oz.						7 oz.	3.5 oz.
Goose liver	0.8	80	180	20	+	?	–	–	?	200	100
	28 oz.	2.8 oz.	6.3 oz.	0.7 oz.						7 oz.	3.5 oz.
Goose gizzards	1.2	80	180	20						200	100
	42 oz.	2.8 oz.	6.3 oz.	0.7 oz.						7 oz.	3.5 oz.
Tripe	1.3	120	250	20	+	+	+	–	?	160	80
	46 oz.	4.2 oz.	8.8 oz.	0.7 oz.						5.6 oz.	2.8 oz.

(The question mark—?—indicates optional ingredients.)

39/a. Tripe pörkölt: Find the ingredients in the chart. Soak the tripe, changing the water a few times. Precook the tripe for an hour (half an hour if you use a pressure cooker). Drain and rinse the precooked tripe, then cut it into strips. Follow the general instructions for *pörkölt,* but use enough water to cover the cooking tripe. This will produce a lot more sauce than usual, which should be thickened by mixing 50 g (½ cup) of flour with cold water to a smooth paste, then slowly adding the paste to the sauce, stirring all the time. Serve the tripe *pörkölt* with boiled potatoes only or potatoes lightly fried with onions.

❧ Meat Dishes ❧

39/b. Puszta pörkölt: Follow Recipe 39 (beef *pörkölt*), but be sure to add marjoram! When the meat is partially cooked, add 1.2 kg (2½–2¾ lb) potatoes, peeled and cut into wedges, along with the cubed tomato and green pepper. Also add at this time 1–2 dl (½–⅞ cup) red wine to the *pörkölt*. This will produce a consistency somewhere between a *gulyás* and *pörkölt*. Finally, before serving, add a few *csipetke* (Recipe 14) to the *pörkölt*. *Puszta pörkölt* is often served in a *bogrács* dish.

40.
Chicken, Veal or Lamb Paprikás

100 g (7 Tbs) lard or shortening	salt
120 g (½ cup) chopped onion	160 g (1 cup) green pepper
12 g (2½ tsp) paprika	80 g (1 medium) tomato (fresh)
2.1 kg (4½–4¾ lb) chicken or	20 g (¼ cup) flour
1.25 kg (2¾ lb) lamb meat with bones,	3 dl (1¼ cups) sour cream
or 1 kg (2¼ lb) boneless veal	

The preparation is very similar to Recipe 39. The difference you can see is that the quantity of lard, onion and paprika is reduced. *Paprikás* has more gravy than *pörkölt*. The onion should be slightly browned to a light yellow color. The major difference comes when the meat is all done; mix the flour and sour cream together and thicken the gravy of the *paprikás* with the mixture while you shake the pot. The preferred accompaniment is small dumplings (*galushka*, Recipe 91), but rice or boiled potatoes are also used. To serve or not to serve a green salad with a dish which has sour cream in it is a matter of individual taste.

We have already described some of the *paprikás* dishes, like Recipe 26 (fish) and 36 (mushroom *paprikás*). Remember, when you prepare these dishes, to review our suggestions about the use of sour cream.

41.
Tokány Debrecen Style

100 g (4 slices) smoked bacon	900 g (2 lb) boneless beef
60 g (6 Tbs) lard	(neck, blade, shin beef)
150 g (⅞ cup) onion	180 g (6 oz) smoked sausage
20 g (4 tsp) paprika	140 g (1 cup) green pepper
salt, garlic	60 g (1 small) fresh tomato

Cut the bacon into small squares and fry until glossy. Add the finely chopped onion and sauté it to a light brown color, stir in the paprika rapidly, and add the meat, cut to finger-sized strips. Add salt and brown the meat, stirring it often. When all the water has evaporated, add a small amount of crushed garlic and a little water or stock. Do not boil the meat, but braise it under a lid. When the meat is partially done (let it cook down to the dripping in the pan), add the smoked sausage rings, the cubed tomato and green pepper, and finish cooking. Serve with rice or *tarhonya* (Recipe 90), or with parsleyed potatoes. Pickles also go well with *tokány*.

42.
Black Pepper Tokány

100 g (7 Tbs) lard	salt, black pepper, garlic
150 g (⅞ cup) onion	140 g (1 cup) green pepper
1 kg (2¼ lb) boneless beef	60 g (1 small) fresh tomato

Follow the recipe for *tokány Debrecen style*, but omit the bacon, paprika and smoked sausage. This *tokány* should have a very pronounced black pepper taste; add enough pepper until it does.

43.
Gundel Tokány

800 g (1¾ lb) beef tenderloin	5 cl (4 Tbs) heavy cream
180 g (6 oz) goose liver	salt, 6 eggs
150 g (1⅓ cups) tender green beans	40 g (3 Tbs) butter
150 g (6 oz) asparagus tips	———
150 g (1 cup) green peas	1 kg (2¼ lb) potatoes
salt, sugar	100 g (7 Tbs) lard
———	———
	30 g (¼ cup) finely chopped onion
100 g (1½ cups) mushrooms	100 g (7 Tbs) lard
20 g (2 Tbs) lard	salt, pepper, marjoram
salt, pepper	15 cl (⅔ cup) red wine
parsley	10 g (2 Tbs) flour

The tenderloin should be aged properly, otherwise do not attempt this recipe. Cut both the tenderloin and the goose liver into thin strips.

Cut the green beans into 2 cm (1 in) pieces; cook the asparagus tips, the green peas and green beans separately (because of their varying cooking times) in salted water. A small amount of sugar can be added to the cooking water.

Sauté the thinly sliced mushrooms in lard with salt, pepper, and chopped parsley until all the water has evaporated.

Make scrambled eggs, using 6 eggs and the cream. Cut the potatoes into very thin julienne pieces and fry in very hot lard.

When this is all done, lightly brown the finely chopped onion in a large frying pan, add the meat, salt, pepper, and a pinch of marjoram. Brown the meat over high heat; shake the pan a few times. When the meat is almost done, add the goose liver and fry that too. Then lower the heat to medium, add the red wine, sprinkle flour over the meat, and stir. Add the mushrooms and the drained cooked vegetables. Let the *tokány* come to a boil once more to let the flavors blend. Serve immediately on an oval dish. Surround the *tokány* with shoe-string potatoes and put the scrambled eggs in the indented center of the *tokány*.

44.
Tokány à la Herány

This dish in one of the favorites of Saxons living in Transylvania.

250 g (½ lb) calf's or pig's kidney
350 g (1¼ cups) small pieces of stewing beef
350 g (1¾ cups) small pieces of stewing pork
180 g (3 cups) mushrooms
————
80 g (6 Tbs) lard
150 g (⅞ cup) onion
15 g (1 Tbs) paprika

marjoram, garlic, salt, pepper
————
80 g (3 slices) smoked bacon
20 g (2 Tbs) lard
salt, pepper
————
20 g (¼ cup) flour
3 dl (1¼ cups) sour cream

Remove the membrane from the kidney, cut it lengthwise, remove all the veins, then scald. Cut the kidney and other meats to small finger-sized strips. Slice the mushrooms into thin slices. Sauté the finely chopped onion until light yellow, stir in the paprika, and immediately add the beef, salt, marjoram, and pepper. Sauté until all the water has evaporated. Then keep on cooking the beef under a lid with the addition of a small amount of stock or water. A very small amount of garlic may also be added. When the beef starts to soften, add the pork. While the beef and pork are cooking, render the small pieces of bacon in a frying pan, add the kidney, mushrooms, salt and pepper to the bacon fat and fry over a fairly high heat. When the meat is just about done, add the contents of the frying pan to the meat. Finish cooking the meat and kidney together. Mix flour into the sour cream and add the mixture to the meat while shaking the pot lightly. Serve potatoes, rice or galushka dumplings (Recipe 91) with this *tokány*.

45.
Seven Chief's Tokány

Named after the chiefs of the seven *Magyar* (Hungarian) tribes who eventually settled the Carpathian Basin after their migrations.

300 g (1¼ cups) stewing beef	12 g (2½ tsp) paprika
300 g (1¼ cups) stewing pork	salt
300 g (1¼ cups) stewing veal	160 g (1 cup) green pepper
100 g (3 slices) smoked bacon	80 g (1 medium) fresh tomato
60 g (¼ cup) lard	20 g (¼ cup) flour
120 g (1 cup) finely chopped onion	2.5 dl (1 cup+2 Tbs) sour cream

Cut the meat to uniform size. Cut the bacon (without its rind) to wide noodle size, wilt in the lard, remove and strain. Sauté the finely chopped onion in drippings. Quickly stir un the paprika and add the beef; salt and brown, until its juice has gone. When the meat is browned, add a small amount of water or stock; cover the pot and braise the beef for about 30 minutes. Then add the pork and braise for an additional 20 minutes, finally adding the veal to the pot. When the meat starts to soften, add the cubed green peppers and tomatoes and the bacon. Mix flour into the sour cream and thicken the gravy with it; shake the pot while you add this mixture. Serve with rice, galushka dumplings (Recipe 91) or *tarhonya* (Recipe 90).

46.
Csikós Tokány

Follow Recipe 45, but use only pork. A small amount of garlic can also be added to this dish.

VII. Stuffed cabbage

47.
Székely Gulyás

Named after József Székely (1825–1895) and not after the ethnic group of the Székelys of Transylvania. József Székely was a writer, journalist, and archivist and the godfather of this tasty *gulyás,* which, however, is not a true *gulyás:* it is thicker and richer, though thinner than a *pörkölt.* Originally three kinds of meat were used for *Székely gulyás,* but nowadays we mostly use pork.

900 g (2 lb) stewing pork	1.2 kg (5 cups) sauerkraut
100 g (7 Tbs) lard	160 g (1 cup) chopped green peppers
250 g (2 cups) chopped onion	20 g (2 Tbs) flour
15 g (1 Tbs) paprika	4 dl (1¾ cups) sour cream
salt, garlic, caraway seeds	fresh dill

Using these ingredients and following Recipe 39, prepare a *pörkölt,* but eliminate or reduce the use of salt.

If the sauerkraut is very salty and sour, rinse it with cold water. If you are not certain, save the water and it can be used later if the flavor is not salty or sour enough.

When the meat is partially cooked, increase the heat in order to evaporate all the water, and add the sauerkraut and green peppers to the meat. Stir in 2 dl (⅞ cup) stock or water, cover the pot and simmer. Do not overcook the sauerkraut; it should be slightly crunchy. Thicken the sauce with the flour–sour cream mixture. After it has boiled, sprinkle finely chopped dill according to taste over the sauerkraut.

Instead of stewing pork, ribs or cutlets can also be used. *Székely gulyás* is very good when reheated, though it loses some of its nutritional value in the process.

VIII. Veal rib Gundel style

48.
Stuffed Cabbage

100 g (½ cup) rice	*1.2 kg (5 cups) sauerkraut*
10 g (1 Tbs) lard or shortening	*6 large or 12 small cabbage leaves*
salt, stock or soup	*200 g (7 oz) smoked meat*
————	*6 g (1.5 tsp) paprika*
100 g (¾ cup) onion	*garlic, pepper*
60 g (¼ cup) lard	————
————	*30 g (2 Tbs) lard*
500 g (2¼ cups) boneless pork, chopped	*20 g (¼ cup) flour*
120 g (4 slices) smoked bacon	*20 g (3 Tbs) chopped onion*
1½ eggs	*1¼ tsp paprika*
pinch of salt, garlic, pepper	————
pinch of marjoram	*10 g (2 Tbs) flour*
5 g (1 tsp) paprika	*3 dl (1¼ cups) sour cream*

Heat 10 g (2 tsp) of lard, add the rice, and an equal volume of water (to each cup of rice, one cup of water). Add the salt and simmer the rice covered until partially cooked. Sauté the finely chopped onion to a light brown color.

When the rice cools down, add it to the chopped meat. Also mix into the meat the bacon cut into small pieces, 1½ eggs and spices.

Prepare the sauerkraut as in Recipe 47. Remove the heavy ribs from the cabbage leaves; they will be more flexible this way. Place equal amounts of the chopped meat mixture on the cabbage leaves. Fold the sides of each leaf over the stuffing and roll the leaves into a cylindrical shape. Fold under the two ends of the rolls with your fingers. Spread two-thirds of the sauerkraut on the bottom of a large pot. Place the stuffed cabbages on the sauerkraut in a single layer, place the smoked meat pieces over the stuffed cabbages, then cover the meat with the left-over sauerkraut. Brown the onion lightly in the lard, add the paprika, then pour it over the sauerkraut. Add enough water or stock to almost cover the sauerkraut. Add a small amount of chopped garlic and pepper. Cover the pot and let simmer for 1–1½ hours over medium heat. Add more water as needed. Remove the stuffed cabbages to a plate and keep them warm. Prepare a light roux with the onion,

lard, paprika and flour. Thicken the sauerkraut with the roux and the flour and sour cream mixture. Bring it to a full boil. Place the stuffed cabbages back on the sauerkraut and serve. You can pour some sour cream over the stuffed cabbage before serving.

48/a. Stuffed Cabbage Kolozsvár Style: Sausage and Canadian bacon and spare-ribs add to the richness of this stuffed cabbage.
Prepare only 6 stuffed cabbages (reduce the stuffing ingredients of Recipe 48 by 20 per cent), replace the bacon and smoked meat with 200 g (6 slices) Canadian style bacon, and 6 links of sausage (Debrecen style), each weighing about 80 g (3 oz). The sausage should be added for only the last 15 minutes of cooking time. When the sauerkraut is ready, fry in hot lard 6 spare-ribs (cutlets) (80 g, 3 oz each). On an oval serving dish first arrange the sauerkraut, top it with the stuffed cabbages, and decorate each stuffing with a piece of Canadian style bacon. On one side of the stuffing place a sausage split in half, and a spare-rib on the other side.
If you want to really decorate your stuffed cabbage platter, slash the edge of the slices of Canadian bacon, fry in lard and sprinkle paprika over them. The fried Canadian bacon will curl up into a ring which should be placed on top of each stuffed cabbage.

48/b. Pork Ribs Hargita Style

720 g (1½ lb) pork ribs (6 slices)	pinch of salt, pepper, marjoram
pinch of salt	6 cabbage leaves
30 g (¼ cup) flour	———
80 g (6 Tbs) lard	150 g (5–6 slices) smoked bacon
———	40 g (3 Tbs) lard
1.2 kg (5 cups) sauerkraut	———
250 g (9 oz) sausage (Debrecen style)	20 g (¼ cup) flour
120 g (1 cup) chopped onion	4 dl (1¾ cups) sour cream
350 g (1½ cups) ground pork	fresh dill

Score the edges of the rib slices, pounding them slightly and salt. Dip the slices into flour and fry them in hot lard. Prepare the sauerkraut as in Recipe 47. Add a small amount of stock or water to the sauerkraut, also add the skinless sausage. When the sausage is done, remove it from the sauerkraut and slice into rings.

Fry the finely chopped onion in the dripping from the pork slices. When the onion is light brown, add the chopped meat and brown it while stirring constantly; add the spices too.

Place a rib-slice on each cabbage leaf, divide the chopped meat in 6 parts and place one on top of each meat slice. Top with sausage rings. Fold the cabbage leaves over and tie each with a common string.

Fry the bacon bits. Pour the dripping and bacon pieces over the sauerkraut. Place the stuffing in a single layer over the sauerkraut. (A tiny bit of garlic could also be added.) Cover the pot. Bake the stuffed cabbage in medium-hot oven for 60–70 minutes. If necessary, add some stock or water. Remove the string from the stuffed cabbage. Thicken the sauerkraut with a flour–sour cream mixture. Reheat the sauerkraut when it has boiled, place the stuffing back on the sauerkraut, spinkle chopped dill over all, and serve very hot.

49.
Mutton with Cabbage

6 portions of mutton pörkölt *600 g (1¼ lb) potatoes*
1 kg (2¼ lb) cabbage *fresh dill, pepper*

To prepare the mutton *pörkölt,* follow Recipe 39. The best cuts of meat for this are the breast or ribs or shoulder. Increase somewhat the quantity of lard, caraway seed and garlic. Cut the cabbage leaves julienne style; cut the potatoes into cubes. When the meat begins to soften, add the cabbage; when that starts to cook, add the potatoes with a small amount of stock or water, and simmer under a lid until all ingredients are cooked. Flavor according to taste with chopped dill and black pepper.

50.
Layered Sauerkraut Transylvania Style

1.2 kg (5 cups) sauerkraut	700 g (1½ lb) fatty pork, salt
———	garlic, pepper, marjoram
150 g (1 cup) onion	150 g (1 package) Canadian bacon (6 slices)
60 g (¼ cup) lard	200 g (7 oz) smoked sausage
10 g (2 tsp) paprika	———
pepper	100 g (⅔ cup) green pepper
———	50 g (1 small) fresh tomato
20 g (1½ Tbs) lard	5 dl (2 cups+2 Tbs) sour cream
150 g (¾ cup) rice	40 g (3 Tbs) lard
———	paprika, parsley

Prepare the sauerkraut as in Recipe 47. Fry the finely chopped onion in lard to a light brown color; quickly add paprika. Add half the fried onion and fat to the sauerkraut, add pepper and stock or water, and simmer for about 15 minutes. Heat the lard or shortening in a pot, add the rice and an equal amount of water (1 cup rice to 1 cup water). Cover and simmer until the rice is partially cooked. Add to the fried onion the chopped meat, salt, garlic, pepper and marjoram. Simmer this mixture over a moderate heat until partially cooked. Fry out the bacon bits, then fry the sausage slices in the bacon dripping.

In a large casserole or roasting pan, make a layer of ⅓ of the sauerkraut with half the rice, meat and sausage. Place half the uncooked cubed green peppers and tomato on top of the sausage slices. Cover with the second ⅓ of the sauerkraut. Pour part of the sour cream over this, then add the remaining half of the rice, meat, sausage, green peppers and tomatoes. Top it off with the last portion of the sauerkraut. Pour sour cream and a small amount of melted lard over the sauerkraut, and sprinkle paprika on top. Cover and bake in a medium-hot oven for 30–40 minutes, then remove the cover for the last 10–20 minutes to brown the top. If necessary, add a small amount of stock or water during the baking time to prevent scorching, but this dish should not have a lot of sauce. Sprinkle the top with finely chopped parsley, cut the layers into squares, and serve very hot. If a Pyrex casserole dish is used to bake the layered sauerkraut, serve it straight from the dish.

51.
Stuffed Green Peppers

For the tomato sauce:	For the stuffing:
100 g (⅔ cup) mixed vegetables	100 g (½ cup) rice
60 g (⅓ cup) chopped onion, celery	10 g (2 tsp) lard
80 g (6 Tbs) lard	(or shortening)
60 g (½ cup) flour	50 g (⅓ cup) onion
1.6 kg (3¼ lb) tomatoes	30 g (2 Tbs) lard, salt
or 350 g (1½ cups) puréed tomatoes	600 g (5½ cups) ground pork
salt	1½ eggs
sugar	salt, small amount of garlic,
	pepper, parsley

12 green peppers

Sauté the mixed vegetables, onion and celery in the lard, sprinkle flour over it and lightly brown. Add the puréed tomatoes, stock or water and spices. Simmer for an hour. Strain the sauce, adjusting the flavoring if necessary. This tomato sauce should be thick and sweet. Select green peppers all about the same size. Cut the tops off and remove the seeds. If the green peppers are hot, scrape out the ribs. If they are very hot, scalding may help. The stuffing is prepared as in Recipe 48, but without the bacon and paprika. A small amount of marjoram may be added to the stuffing. Mix the stuffing well and fill each green pepper; do not try to overstuff them. Place the stuffed green peppers in a large enough pot for them to be in a single layer. Pour the tomato sauce over the stuffed green peppers. Cover the pot and cook over a low heat. Shake the pot from time to time. Serve with parsleyed boiled potatoes.

Stuffed green pepper variations: instead of tomato sauce, dill sauce may be used, and instead of the traditional meat, you can stuff the green peppers with rice mixed with chopped ham, eggs or green peas. (*Make the dill sauce* by preparing a roux, adding the chopped dill, diluting with cold liquid and adding sour cream.)

52.
Pörkölt of Sirloin

1 kg (2¼ lb) boneless sirloin	60 g (5 Tbs) lard
(cut in thin slices)	250 g (1½ cups) onion
salt	20 g (4 tsp) paprika
60 g (½ cup) flour	garlic, caraway seeds
60 g (5 Tbs) lard	160 g (1 cup) green peppers
———	80 g (⅓ cup) fresh tomatoes

Pound the slices until thin; score them at the edges. Dip the slices in flour and brown in hot lard on both sides. Transfer the browned slices to a large saucepan. Add more lard to the frying pan, brown the finely chopped onions to a light brown color, mix in the paprika rapidly, and add water or stock. When this mixture boils, pour it over the browned meat slices. Add the crushed garlic and caraway seeds and simmer covered over medium heat. Shake the saucepan from time to time. If necessary, add small quantities of water; the meat should be almost frying. When the meat is partially cooked, add the cubed tomatoes and green peppers. Serve with boiled potatoes, galushka dumplings (Recipe 91) or *tarhonya* (Recipe 90).

52/a. Sirloin Steaks Hortobágy Style: The only difference between this version and basic Recipe 52 is that the *Hortobágy* style sirloin is served with a semolina dumpling on each slice of meat. Prepare the *semolina dumplings* while the meat is cooking. Combine 50 g (5 Tbs) lard, and 1 egg yolk until foamy. Add salt and 120 g (¾ cup) semolina. Let the mixture rest ½ hour. Whip the egg white until stiff but not dry, then carefully fold it into the semolina mixture. Boil salted water in a pot, dip a large spoon in the boiling water, take a spoonful of the semolina mixture and drop it into the boiling water; repeat the process. When the dumpling is done, you can let it stand in the water for a while but not for too long.
To serve, place a dumpling on each side of meat and pour the gravy over the dumplings. Sprinkle with chopped parsley.

52/b. Sirloin Steaks in Lecsó: Omit the caraway seeds, tomatoes and green peppers from Recipe 52. Following Recipe 83 for *lecsó* using 100 g (3 slices) smoked bacon, 1 kg (2¼ lb) of green peppers, 400 g (5 small) tomatoes to prepare the *lecsó*. When the sirloin steaks are partially done, pour *lecsó*

over them and finish cooking the *lecsó* and sirloin together. Accompany this dish with boiled potatoes; do not serve pickles with it.

52/c. Sirloin Steaks Szeged Style: Prepare the sirloin steaks as in Recipe 52. Prepare soup pasta *(csipetke)* as in Recipe 14. Peel and cube 150 g (1 cup) carrots, 100 g (½ cup) parsley roots, 50 g (¼ cup) celeriac, 1 kg (2¼ lb) potatoes. The potatoes should be cut into larger cubes than the rest of the vegetables. Braise all the vegetables in small amount of lard.
When the sirloin steaks are partially done, add a small amount of water or stock. When serving the sirloin steaks *Szeged* style, first place the meat on the serving plate, then place the vegetables on the meat; the *csipetke* follows the vegetables, and finally the sauce. Sprinkle with finely chopped parsley.

52/d. Serbian Sirloin Steaks: Follow Recipe 52 until the last steps. While the meat is cooking, fry out 60 g (2 slices) bacon cubes, partially cook 800 g (1¾ lb) Savoy cabbage in salted water; peel and cube 1 kg (2¼ lb) of potatoes. When the meat is partially cooked, drain and cut the Savoy cabbage into segments and add it to the meat. Also add the potatoes, bacon, green pepper and tomatoes. Continue cooking until all ingredients are tender.

52/e. Sirloin Steaks Style: Follow Recipe 52, but omit the garlic and caraway seeds, and reduce the lard, onion and paprika by 30 per cent. While the meat is cooking, score and fry 6 bacon slices until golden brown. Drain the bacon drippings over the meat. When the meat is tender, mix 20 g (½ cup) flour with 2 dl (3¼ lb) sour cream and stir the mixture into the sauce. When serving, place a slice of fried bacon on top of each steak. Serve with galushka dumplings.

52/f. Sirloin Steaks in a Pan: The only difference between this recipe and 52 is that when the meat is partially cooked, we add 1.5 kg (3¼ lb) potatoes cut into segments and some stock or water to the meat along with the green peppers and tomatoes.

52/g. Sirloin Steaks with Smoked Sausage: While the meat is cooking, cook 200 g (7 oz) of smoked sausage *(Debreceni)* for 10 minutes with the meat. Remove the sausage; peel and slice it. Along with the green peppers and tomatoes, add to the meat 1.2 kg (2½–2¾ lb) potato segments and

water or stock to cover the potatoes. Fry until slightly brown 100 g (3 slices) bacon bits; add the sausage slices to the bacon dripping and fry them for a few minutes.

Pour the bacon bits, dripping and sausage slices over the meat. Cook for the flavors to blend.

52/h. Sirloin Steaks Casino Style: Prepare the meat according to Recipe 52. Peel and cut 1 kg (2¼ lb) potatoes into 12 or more rectangular shapes (like dominoes). Boil the potatoes. Cook 200 g (1⅓ cups) green peas. Boil 6 hard-boiled eggs. Peel the eggs. Keep all warm in their cooking liquids. When serving, place a slice of meat on the plate, place 2 slices of potatoes on the meat, and on each slice of potato place half a hard-boiled egg. Decorate the plates with green peas and finely chopped parsley.

53.
Chef Csáky's Sirloin

Named after Master Chef Sándor Csáky, author of the cookbook *The Art of Cooking in the 20th Century* (in Hungarian).

1 kg (2¼ lb) boneless sirloin	*10 g (2 tsp) paprika*
(3–6 slices), salt, pepper	————
————	*160 g (1 cup) green pepper*
3 portions of lecsó prepared	*80 g (⅓ cup) tomatoes*
with 100 g (3 slices) of smoked bacon	————
6 eggs	*20 g (½ cup) flour*
salt	*3 dl (1¼ cups) sour cream*
120 g (½ cup) lard	*parsley*
180 g (1⅓ cups) onion	*6 butter dumplings*

Cut the sirloin almost through, open and pound thin. Sprinkle salt and pepper on each slice. Prepare *lecsó* according to Recipe 83 using only half the ingredients, but doubling the amount of bacon. Chop the onion finely, cube the tomatoes and green peppers. When these ingredients are properly stewed, mix in the eggs and salt and finish cooking. The *lecsó* will solidify rapidly.

Divide the *lecsó*–egg mixture evenly and spread it on the meat slices. Fold over the sides of the meat and roll the slices up; tie each cylinder with cotton string. Place the meat rolls in a baking dish with some lard and bake for about 15 minutes. Turn a few times, then transfer the meat to a saucepan. Fry the finely chopped onion in the lard, add the paprika, stir vigorously, quickly add water or stock and pour over the meat. Cover and simmer the meat over medium heat. Add water or stock if necessary. When the meat is partially cooked, add the tomatoes and green peppers. When it is completely cooked, remove the strings from the meat rolls, place them on a platter and keep them warm. Combine the flour and sour cream, stir into the sauce in the saucepan, and boil. Cut the meat rolls diagonally and strain the gravy over them; sprinkle with chopped parsley.

To prepare the butter dumplings mix 120 g (½ cup+1 Tbs) butter with 2 egg yolks until creamy, add salt and 300 g (2⅔ cups) flour with semolina (like Wondra), whip the egg whites until fluffy and add them to the mixture. Boil salted water in a pot, dip a large spoon in the boiling water, take a spoonful of the dumpling batter and drop it into the water. If the first dumpling falls apart, add more flour, if it is too firm, add a bit of water or butter to the batter. Cook until tender.

54.
Steak Esterházy

Named after the diplomat and politician Prince Pál Antal Esterházy (1786–1866), who represented Hungary at the Court of St. James's. He was a member of the Batthyány government in 1848, and a member of the Hungarian Academy of Sciences.

1 kg (2¼ lb) boneless sirloin slices, salt	salt, pepper
60 g (½ cup) flour	1 dl (7 Tbs) wine
60 g (¼ cup) lard	peel of 1 lemon
———	1 bay leaf, 20 capers
150 g (1¼ cups) carrots	30 g (2 Tbs) mustard (prepared)
100 g (½ cup) parsley root	
50 g (½ cup) celery	20 g (2½ Tbs) of flour
80 g (⅔ cup) onion	3 dl (1½ cups) sour cream
100 g (7 Tbs) lard	lemon juice, sugar, parsley

Pre-fry the steaks as in Recipe 52. Julienne the vegetables, finely chop the onion, add lard to the frying pan and lightly brown the vegetables and onion; add salt and pepper while browning. Add a small amount of stock (or water) and the wine to the vegetables and bring to a boil. Strain over the steaks, reserving the vegetables. Add to the meat the lemon peel, bay leaf, chopped capers and mustard; cover and simmer. When the meat is partially cooked add the vegetables and finish cooking.

Remove the lemon peel and bay leaf. Combine the sour cream and flour and stir into the gravy while you shake the pot slightly. Adjust the flavoring with the addition of lemon juice and sugar and bring the dish to a boil one more time. On serving, sprinkle chopped parsley over the meat; accompany with galushka dumplings (Recipe 109), rice or spaghetti.

55.
Fillet of Beef Budapest Style

1 kg (2¼ lb) beef fillet	300 g (½–¾ lb) veal or pork bones
prepared mustard, oil, pepper	150 g (1 cup) green peppers
———	150 g (2 cups) mushrooms
3 portions of boiled rice	150 g (1 cup) goose liver
———	80 g (3 slices) smoked bacon
60 g (¼ cup) lard	30 g (2 Tbs) lard
120 g (¾ cup) onion	———
10 g (2 tsp) paprika	150 g (1 cup) green peas, salt
30 g (2 Tbs) tomato paste, salt	120 g (½ cup) lard

Use properly aged beef for this dish. Marinate 6 slices of the fillet in mustard, oil and pepper in the refrigerator for several days.

Prepare 3 portions of boiled rice. Meanwhile, lightly brown the chopped onion in the lard, add the paprika and tomato paste and stir, then immediately add about 3 dl (1¼ cups) water, salt and the bones. Boil for half an hour to prepare a *pörkölt* sauce. Remove the bones and strain the sauce. Cut the green peppers, mushrooms, goose liver and bacon into squares. Wilt the bacon in a small amount of lard, then add the rest of the cut ingredients and fry them together. Pour the *pörkölt* over the fried ingredients. Simmer to blend the flavors in the gravy.

Cook the green peas in a small amount of salted water. Just before serving, panfry the fillet steaks medium to medium rare, sprinkle salt over the fried fillet, place them on a bed of rice, pour the sauce over them, pour the drained green peas on top. Serve with deep-fried potatoes.

56.
Veal Roll with Ham

300 g (½–¾ lb) uncooked smoked ham	pepper, nutmeg, salt
1 kg (2¼ lb) boneless veal, salt	60 g (½ cup) flour
———	60 g (¼ cup) lard
For the Bechamel sauce:	
50 g (¼ cup) butter	60 g (¼ cup) lard
40 g (6 Tbs) flour	150 g (⅞ cup) onion
3 dl (1¼ cups) milk	15 g (1 Tbs) paprika
30 g (¼ cup) cheese	30 g (2 Tbs) tomato paste
1 egg yolk	100 g (⅔ cup) green peppers

Cook the smoked ham or other not too fatty smoked meat until tender, then chop it finely. Cut the veal into 6 large slices, pound them thin, score the edges and salt the veal slightly. Prepare the *Bechamel sauce:* heat the butter, mix in the flour, making sure that it will not brown; slowly add the milk, stir continuously, add the flavoring and simmer for about half an hour. Mix the ham and grated cheese with the egg yolk and pepper, strain the sauce through cheese cloth and mix well into a paste. Spread the paste over the 6 slices of veal, roll them up like French crepes and tie with cotton string. Dip the meat rolls in flour and brown them in hot lard. When browned, place the meat rolls in a larger pot. Brown a chopped onion in some lard in a frying pan, and paprika and tomato paste and a small amount of the cooking stock of the ham. You may also add a small amount of garlic. Pour this mixture over the meat, cover and simmer. If necessary, add more ham stock; if it is too salty, add part water. When the meat is partially cooked, add the green pepper. Before serving, remove the strings, place the meat rolls on a platter and pour the sauce over them. Serve with mashed potatoes or galushka dumplings, and pickles.

✳ Meat Dishes ✳

57.
Pittsburgh Veal Chops

Károly Gundel created this dish in honor of the Mayor of Pittsburgh when he visited Budapest. It has remained on the Gundel menu ever since.

6 portions of brown (Spanish) gravy	*For the goose liver purée:*
———	*50 g (½ cup) onion*
6 pieces 180 g (7 oz) veal rib chops	*50 g (¼ cup) lard*
or, if you prefer, 12 smaller size	*360 g (¾ lb) goose or duck liver*
100 g (4 oz) rib chops, salt	*salt*
———	*black pepper*
60 g (½ cup) flour	*cayenne pepper*
80 g (6 Tbs) butter	*20 g (¼ cup) flour*
———	*1 dl (7 Tbs) milk*
60 g (¼ cup) ham	*1 egg*
120 g (2 cups) mushrooms	*2 cl (1½ Tbs) brandy*
1 dl (7 Tbs) red wine	*1 dl (7 Tbs) whipped cream (unsweetened)*

Prepare or purchase the brown gravy a day before use. Cut a slit in the center of each rib chop, making an opening just as wide as the blade of the knife. Salt the chops.

To make the *goose liver purée:* fry finely chopped onion in the lard to a light yellow color, add diced liver, salt, pepper, cayenne pepper (or a paté spice mixture) and simmer until the liver is done. Sprinkle flour over it, pour the milk into the mixture, stir and bring to the boil. Reduce the meat, add the egg (do not boil any more) and the brandy. Press this mixture through a sieve. Add the unsweetened whipped cream to the liver to produce a light purée. Use a pastry bag to fill the rib chops with the paté. Fasten the openings with meat pins. Dip the chops in flour and brown them in a small amount of hot butter. When both sides are browned, add about 3 dl (1¼ cups) stock. Cover and simmer until the meat is tender. Meanwhile, julienne the ham and mushrooms and add to the brown gravy. Thin the gravy with red wine and bring to a boil. When the meat is tender, pour the gravy over it and serve with creamed corn (Recipe 89) or fried potatoes.

58.
Hungarian Veal Medallions

1 kg (2¼ lb) veal for cutlets	15 g (3 tsp) paprika, salt
salt	50 g (½ cup) flour
———	120 g (½ cup) lard
1.5 kg (3¼ lb) potatoes, salt	———
———	250 g (1⅔ cups) green pepper
150 g (1 cup) onion	120 g (½ cup) fresh tomatoes
80 g (6 Tbs) lard	parsley

Trim the meat and cut it into 20–30 g (1 oz) slices. Lightly pound the slices. Boil the potatoes. When the potatoes are almost done, peel and slice them. Lightly brown the finely chopped onion in the lard, add paprika and a small amount of stock or water and salt to taste. Boil until the onion is soft. Dip the meat slices in flour and brown them in a small amount of lard, over high heat. When the slices are golden brown, place them in the sauce, add green peppers and tomatoes, cover and simmer until the meat is tender. Meanwhile, brown the potato slices in the dripping, turning and shaking until they become nicely colored. When the meat is done, add the potatoes to it, bring to a boil once more, and sprinkle with chopped parsley before serving.

59.
Veal Rib Chops Gundel Style

Follow Recipe 29 for Pike or Perch Gundel Style, but substitute six 150 g (5 oz) slices of veal cutlets (boned or boneless) for the fish. Also, add 100 g (¾ cup) finely julienned smoked cooked ham to the sauce.

60.
Veal Cutlet Magyaróvár Style

This veal dish was created by János Rákóczi, the former chef of the Gundel restaurant in the Gellért Hotel, for the 1958 World Fair at Brussels. Besides Mr. Rákóczi, six other former Gundel chefs were employed at the World Fair.

840 g (1¾–2 lb) veal cutlets	salt, pepper, parsley
———	———
250 g (3½ cups) mushrooms	1 kg (2¼ lb) potatoes
50 g (¼ cup) butter	———
30 g (2½ Tbs) onion	50 g (½ cup) flour
salt, pepper, parsley, 1 egg	100 g (½ cup) lard
———	
200 g (1 cup) rice	180 g (4 x 1½ slices) cooked ham
salt	100 g (4 x 1½ slices) semi-soft cheese
———	(like Port-Salut)
150 g (1 cup) fresh green peas	———
120 g (½ cup) fresh tomatoes	20 g (2 Tbs) butter
40 g (3 Tbs) butter	150 g (⅔ cup) lard (for the potatoes)

Pound the meat slices, score the edges and salt them. Prepare a mushroom paste according to Recipe 21, but bind it with an egg instead of mayonnaise. Beat the egg lightly, then add it to the hot mushrooms in a steady light stream, mixing rapidly. If the paste is not thick enough, add some breadcrumbs.

Steam the rice. Cook the green peas in a small amount of salted water. Brown the diced tomatoes in the butter and add salt, pepper and parsley to it. When the green peas are soft, drain. Add the cooked tomatoes and drained peas to the cooked rice. Julienne the potatoes and fry as shoe-string potatoes.

Dip the meat in flour and brown it in the hot lard until it is reddish brown. Spread the mushroom paste on the meat slices, top each with a slice of ham and cheese, and grill until the cheese is melted. Place the meat on a bed of rice and surround with fried shoe-string potatoes. Pour the dripping (after the addition of a bit of butter) over the meat just before serving.

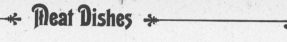

✳ Meat Dishes ✳

61.
Steak à la Feszty

Named to honor the painter Árpád Feszty (1856–1914).

Use well aged beef steak for this recipe. Do not pound the steaks flat. They should weigh at least 220 g (8 oz) each. Three or four days before you want to enjoy or serve Steak à la Feszty, spread mustard on each steak, dip the steaks in oil, sprinkle with freshly ground pepper. Place the steak slices on top of each other, and marinate in the refrigerator. When you are ready to fry the steaks, sprinkle them on both sides with a salt–paprika mixture. Cut diagonal slits about half way into the steaks. Peel a large onion, but do not slice it since slices tend to fall apart. Instead, peel pieces off. Place slices of bacon and pieces of onion into the slits. Secure the bacon and onion by tying a cotton string around the steaks. Grill the steaks rare, otherwise the edge of the onion pieces will burn. Toast 6 roll slices. Top the toast rounds with steak. For an accompaniment use fried potatoes, mashed potatoes, steamed vegetables, or anything else you like to have with steak.

62.
Pork Chops Hungarian Style

Prepare the pork chops according to Recipes 52/b, c, f or g for sirloin steaks, or Recipe 47 for Székely gulyás.

IX. Mixed grill on a wooden platter
X. Turkey with goose liver and chestnut stuffing

63.
Quick-Fried Pork Chops Torda Style

1.2 kg (1½–1¾ lb) young pork loin (with skin on)	5 g (1 tsp) paprika
salt	40 g (6 Tbs) flour
————	1.8 kg (4 lb) potatoes
4 portions of mixed salad	200 g (⅞ cup) lard for the potatoes
	100 g (7 Tbs) lard for the meat

The pork loin should be aged for a few days in the refrigerator. Sear and scrape the skin. Cut into 12 slices. Pound the slices and score the edges. Salt the meat.

Use a large platter (wood if you have it). Decorate the edge with nicely arranged salads, for example: pickled beet slices, marinated green peppers, tomatoes, sliced gherkins, lettuce, coleslaw. Keep the platter chilled.

Just before serving time, dip the meat into a flour and paprika mixture and fry over high heat in lard. In another frying pan prepare the French fried potatoes. Pile the potatoes in the center of the platter, and salt them. Surround the potatoes with the fried pork chops.

64.
Hungarian Mixed Grill

This version of a mixed grill (fatányéros) first appeared on the menu around 1900. But our ancestors too sometimes used a freshly cut wood plank as a platter on which to eat food fried over a camp fire.

Today we use a grooved wooden plate which is often placed over a silver platter to serve an elegant version of grilled meats. The preparation is very similar to the quick-fried pork loin chops, Recipe 63, except that a variety of meats is used. For each person prepare 1 slice 100 g (3½ oz) of pork chop, 60 g (2 oz) veal chop, 60 g (2 oz) sirloin steak, 30 g (1 oz) goose liver slice, and 30 g (1 oz) (1 slice) bacon. Score the bacon so it will curl up nicely. Grill all the meat until tender. Place on the decorative platter and top with bacon curls. Offer a small knife decorated with Hungarian motifs, or one that resembles a jack-knife, to each guest.

Meat Dishes

65.
Sour Pork

1 kg (2¼ lb) boneless young pork or 1.5 kg (3¼ lb) pork with bones	30 g (¼ cup) flour
	2 dl (⅞ cup) sour cream
	20 g (4 tsp) prepared mustard
80 g (1 Tbs) lard	10 g (1 Tbs) sugar
60 g (⅓ cup) onion	5 cl (4 Tbs) lemon juice
salt, pepper, bay leaf	lemon peel

Sear the skin and scrape it clean. Cut the boneless meat into 20–30 g (1 oz) pieces. Cut the bony meat to larger 40–50 g (1½–2 oz) pieces.

Heat the lard in a pot, fry the onion lightly, add the meat and spices, cover and cook on medium heat with the addition of a small amount of stock or water. When the meat is almost tender, mix the flour and sour cream and add it to the meat. For flavoring use the mustard, sugar, lemon juice and a small amount of grated lemon peel. Finely chopped pickled tarragon leaves may also be used. The flavoring should be done in several steps, checking to make sure that the meat has a piquant taste. Serve with boiled potatoes or rice.

66.
Lamb with Tarragon

1.5 kg (3¼ lb) suckling lamb (neck, shoulder, breast or shank)	40 g (6 Tbs) flour
	2 dl (⅞ cup) sour cream
80 g (½ cup) onion	½ dl (4 Tbs) lemon juice
salt, pepper	tarragon vinegar
20 g (4 tsp) pickled tarragon or	10 g (2 tsp) sugar
5 g (1 tsp) fresh tarragon leaf	1 dl (7 Tbs) cream
80 g (6 Tbs) butter	1 egg yolk

Remove the larger bones and use them to make a stock. The rest of the meat should be cut up as in the previous recipe. Cook the cut up meat with an onion, salt and peppercorns in the strained stock. When the meat is almost tender, remove the onion, add the finely minced tarragon and

thicken with a light butter roux. The gravy should have the consistency of a cream soup. Add the sour cream (if necessary, with some flour); also add tarragon vinegar, lemon juice and sugar in small portions, tasting each time to obtain a piquant flavor. Simmer to blend the flavors. Remove the meat to a serving bowl and keep it warm. Beat the egg yolk and cream together, and add it to the sauce in a slow, steady stream, making sure that it does not boil again. Pour the sauce over the meat. Serve with rice or parsleyed potatoes.

67.
Mutton Rib Chops Udvarhely Style

500 g (6 small) fresh tomatoes
600 g (1¼ lb) string beans, salt

5 g (1 tsp) paprika
1 clove of garlic

120 g (4 slices) smoked bacon
40 g (3 Tbs) lard
60 g (⅓ cup) onion,
salt, pepper

1.2 kg (2½–2¾ lb) lamb chops
salt, pepper
80 g (6 Tbs) lard
parsley

Scald and peel the tomatoes, then cube them. Cut the string beans into 2 cm (¾ in) pieces, and cook in salted water. Cut the bacon to small squares and wilt in a small amount of lard. Add the finely chopped onion to the bacon and brown to a light brown color. Now add the cubed tomatoes, spices and simmer for a while, then add the cooked string beans.
Cut 12 chops from the meat. Sprinkle salt and pepper on the chops. Fry until pink on the inside. Pour the string bean sauce over the chops, sprinkle with chopped parsley and serve with French fried potatoes.

Meat Dishes

68.
Turkey with Goose Liver and Chestnut Stuffing

600 g (1¼ lb) chestnut	120 g (½ cup) lard
2 dl (¾ cup) red wine	———
———	12 apples Bayard style
2 hard rolls	(Recipe 93)
1.5 dl (⅔ cup) heavy cream	———
———	For the goose liver paté:
1 turkey (3.5 kg, 7½ lb)	40 g (¼ cup) onion
180 g (6 slices) bacon	40 g (3 Tbs) lard
salt	250 g (1⅔ cups) goose
marjoram	or duck liver
———	salt, pepper, cayenne pepper
300 g (10 oz) stewing veal	15 g (2 Tbs) flour
2 eggs	1.5 dl (⅔ cup) milk
salt, pepper, parsley, nutmeg	1 small egg
80 g (6 Tbs) butter	1 cl (1 Tbs) brandy
———	1 dl (7 Tbs) heavy cream

Score the shells of the chestnuts and bake them on a cookie sheet until partially done. Remove both the outside shell and inside skin. Finish cooking the chestnuts in the red wine. They should absorb all the wine by the time they are cooked. Soak the rolls in the sweet cream.

Remove the wings and legs from a young plump turkey. Pull the heavy tendons off the drumsticks. Lard the turkey breast and drumsticks with bacon. Sprinkle salt and marjoram in the cavity. Grind the veal and soaked roll together (use a rough grinder); add the egg, minced chestnuts, spices, parsley and melted butter to the veal and roll; mix all together. Stuff the turkey and truss it. Pour some melted lard over the turkey and bake it in a medium hot oven, basting periodically, until tender and nicely browned (about 2 hours).

While the turkey is in the oven, prepare the apples Bayard style (Recipe 93) and the goose liver purée according to Recipe 57. When the turkey is done, carefully remove the breast and the breast

bone using poultry shears. Discard the bone. Slice the meat diagonally and place it carefully back on the turkey. Decorate it with liver paté pushed through a pastry bag. Reheat the turkey if necessary. Serve with baked potatoes, rice, apple sauce, stewed prunes or apples.

69.
Stuffed Chicken Transylvanian Style

2 hard rolls	————
2 dl (⅞ cup) milk, 2 eggs	*2 eggs*
	80 g (6 Tbs) butter
————	
180 g (1¼ cups) goose liver	
180 g (2½ cups) mushrooms	*salt*
150 g (1 package) smoked bacon	*marjoram*
50 g (⅓ cup) onion	*2–2.1 kg (4½ lb) chicken*
50 g (¼ cup) butter	————
salt, pepper, parsley	*100 g (7 Tbs) lard*

Soak the rolls in the milk. Hard-boil the eggs. Cube the goose liver, mushrooms and bacon. Fry out the bacon; fry the chopped onion to a light color in the bacon dripping, then add the mushrooms. Cook until the water has evaporated. Add the goose liver and seasonings and brown lightly. Cool the mixture.

To stuff: Mix the butter and egg until creamy, add the squeezed out rolls, the cubed hard-boiled eggs, and lastly, the goose liver mixture. Mix all the ingredients well. Salt the chicken, sprinkle the inside of the chicken with marjoram and stuff it with the dressing. Truss the chicken, pour melted lard over it and bake it in a medium hot oven. Serve it with baked potatoes, rice, green peas or lettuce.

70.
Goose Giblets with Rice

2.8 kg (6–6¼ lb) gizzards from 3 geese	salt, pepper, marjoram
———	100 g (1½ cups) mushrooms
100 g (¾ cup) carrots	20 g (2 Tbs) goose fat
80 g (¾ cup) parsley roots	salt, pepper, parsley
60 g (⅔ cup) celeriac	
100 g (⅔ cup) green peppers	360 g (2 cups) rice
50 g (1 small) fresh tomato	40 g (4 Tbs) goose fat
150 g (1¼ cups) fresh green peas	———
salt	300 g (½–¾ lb) goose liver
———	salt, pepper
60 g (6 Tbs) goose fat	30 g (¼ cup) flour
30 g (3 Tbs) onion	20 g (2 Tbs) goose fat

Clean the heads, wings, giblets, legs; scald to be able to remove heavy skins and claws. Cut each meat piece into 2 parts, cut the vegetables into large cubes, the tomatoes and green peppers into smaller ones. Cook the green peas in salted water.

Wilt finely chopped onion in lard, add the vegetables; when they start to brown, add the meat and spices. Add a small amount of water as it becomes necessary, and simmer the meat under a lid. Meanwhile, brown the sliced mushrooms in lard seasoned with salt, pepper and parsley. Shake the pot (don't stir) while the mushrooms are browning. Slightly brown the rice for a few minutes in lard (in a separate pot). When the meat begins to turn tender, reduce the cooking liquid until the meat begins to fry. Add the rice, mushrooms, green peppers and tomatoes to the meat; add water (twice the volume of the rice used). Mix all ingredients well and cover. Place in a medium hot oven for about 20 minutes or until the rice and meat are tender. Meanwhile salt and pepper 6 slices of goose liver, dip them in flour and fry them in hot lard. Decorate the rice with the fried liver slices, you can also pour the liver dripping over the rice. Some people like to have grated cheese or ketchup with this dish, whereas others serve it with pickles.

71.
Goose in a Pan

Prepared just like sirloin steak in a pan (Recipe 52/f) but from 2 kg (4½ lb) of goose meat, no additional lard is necessary. Just use the goose fat, and do not dip the meat into flour before it is prefried. It can be prepared from selected parts, or any other parts deboned, the fatty parts fried separately.

72.
Venison or Rabbit Slices à la Kedvessy

Nándor Kedvessy (1869–1960) was a well known restaurateur and chef, the creator of this dish.

2 kg (4¼–4½ lb) venison	2 dl (¾ cup) white wine
or rabbit with bones	5 cl (4 Tbs) brandy
salt, pepper	2 dl (¾ cup) heavy cream
———	15 g (2 Tbs) flour, 30 g (2 Tbs) butter
12 mushroom caps	lemon juice, salt
12 slices of rolls	———
300 g (1½ cups) rice	150 g (½ cup − 2 Tbs) lard
———	salt, pepper, parsley

Age the meat for a few days in the refrigerator. A day before cooking remove the bones and skin. Pound the slices lightly, salt and pepper them. Boil the bones in water; reduce the stock to about 1 dl (6 Tbs).

Next day wash the mushroom caps, cut slices of roll about 8 mm (⅓ in) thick, trim them to the same size as the meat slices. Prepare the rice, then the sauce. *For the sauce,* boil the wine and brandy, add the sweet cream and stock, knead the flour and butter together and sprinkle the mixture on the sauce to thicken it. Flavor the sauce with lemon juice and salt; whisk until smooth.

Salt and pepper the mushroom caps and brown them in a little lard. Keep them warm. Press the hot rice in a preheated bowl and invert it over a large hot platter. Decorate the rice with chopped parsley. Use the dripping to toast the sliced rolls; when toasted, place around the rice. Fry the meat in lard until the inside just turns pink. Place 1 slice of venison or 2–3 slices of rabbit on each piece of toast; top with a mushroom cap. Mix all or just part of the dripping with the sauce and pour over the meat. Serve immediately.

73.
Pheasant or Partridge with Savoy Cabbage

This is one of the fall favorites the Gundel Restaurant serves at the City Park.

2 pheasants or 6 partridges	*80 g (6 Tbs) lard*
salt, marjoram	*250 g (9 oz) smoked sausage*
80 g (6 Tbs) lard	
———	———
1.8 kg (4 lb) Savoy cabbage	*200 g (½ lb/1½ cups) carrots*
salt, 60 g (1 large) onion	*200 g (½ lb/2 cups) parsley roots*
250 g (9 oz) Canadian bacon (6 slices)	*pepper*
	20 g (2 Tbs) butter

You can use older birds for this dish. Age the birds for a few days; clean them before or after aging. When ready to cook, salt them and sprinkle marjoram in the cavity and simmer in a small amount of lard until tender. Meanwhile, cut out the core of the Savoy cabbage and cut the rest of it into segments. Cook the cabbage in a pot of boiling water with a large onion until half tender, then discard the onion and drain the cabbage segments. Save the cooking water.

Cut the partridges into quarters; bone the pheasants and slice the breasts.

Fry out 6 slices of the Canadian bacon. Remove the fried bacon and use the dripping to fry the smoked sausage which should be split lengthwise first and have its skin removed. Remove the fried sausage. In the dripping, sauté the vegetables which should be cut with a serrated knife into fancy rings. When the vegetables are nicely colored, remove them and finish cooking in a small amount of the cooking water of the cabbage. Braise the Savoy cabbage until tender in the remaining lard, with a lot of pepper. Take 6 serving bowls, butter them, place 1 slice of the fried Canadian bacon in the center. On the sides, place the fried sausage slices (2 in each bowl), surround this with a vegetable ring, alternating carrots with parsley roots. Place some of the Savoy cabbage on the bacon, then some of the meat, then drippings, then cabbage again. Steam the bowls in the oven. Preheat 6 plates, invert a bowl over each plate, pour some hot dripping over the cabbage and serve.

74.
Stuffed Pheasant à la Széchenyi

Named after Count István Széchenyi (1791–1860), who played an important role in the liberal reform movement in Hungary. He established the Hungarian Academy of Sciences, wrote books and was a politician. He earned the title of the "Greatest Hungarian" of his time.

240 g (½ lb) goose liver	240 g (½ lb) mushrooms
salt, spices for paté	———
5 cl (4 Tbs) Tokay wine	300 g (1⅔ cups) steamed rice
(heavy white wine)	50 g (¼ cup) lard
3 cl (3 Tbs) brandy	———
———	1 kg (2 ¼ lb) chestnut
2 young pheasants	60 g (¼ cup) butter
salt, marjoram	2 dl (¾ cup) heavy cream
———	10 g (1 Tbs) sugar, salt
180 g (6 slices) smoked bacon	2 blood oranges
100 g (½ cup) lard	

The day before you prepare this dish slice the liver into 20 g (1 oz) slices. Marinate the slices in wine and brandy, with the addition of spices and salt.

When you clean the pheasants, make sure the skin remains intact. Insert the marinated liver slices under the pheasant skin, over the breasts and drumsticks. Save the marinade. Tie the bacon over the pheasant breasts, salt the birds and sprinkle marjoram over them. Bake the pheasants in hot lard, adding water as needed, in a hot oven. Baste occasionally. Fry the salted mushroom caps. Cook the rice. Cook and peel the chestnuts. Rice the chestnuts meats or press through a fine sieve; mix with butter, sweet cream, a small amount of salt and sugar, and simmer until smooth. If necessary, add some milk.

Place the rice on a platter. Remove the string from the pheasants, cut into serving pieces and slice the breasts. Place the meat on the rice, topping it with the breast and bacon slices. Surround the rice with the mushroom caps and edge the platter with orange slices cut in half. Simmer the marinade and drippings together and pour it over the meat.

Serve the hot puréed chestnuts in a side dish.

Meat Dishes

75.
Wild Board Gourmet Style

1.5 kg (3¼ lb) wild board meat with bones, garlic, salt, pepper	50 g (1 small) tomato
	40 g (3 Tbs) butter
	parsley
———	2 dl (¾ cup) red wine
150 g (6 oz) smoked tongue bay leaf, peppercorn	3 g (1 tsp) paprika
	black pepper
———	30 g (2 Tbs) red current jelly or puréed cranberry
5 dl (1 pt) brown gravy	10 g (2 tsp) prepared mustard
———	2 cl (2 Tbs) lemon juice,
120 g (2 medium) sour gherkins	thyme, Juniper berries
120 g (2 cups) mushrooms	10 g (2 Tbs) flour
100 g (⅔ cup) green pepper	

A day before you want to serve the wild boar, carefully remove all bristle and bone. Leave the skin intact. Rub the meat with garlic, or spread chopped garlic over it. Salt and pepper the meat lightly. Roll and tie up. Cook the bones and smoked tongue with the bay leaf and peppercorn until it is soft. Prepare the brown (Spanish) gravy.

Next day remove the bones from the stock. Remove the skin of the tongue. Boil the meat in the stock; let the stock reduce. Meanwhile, julienne the tongue, mushrooms and sour gherkins. Dice the green peppers and tomatoes. Brown the mushroom and parsley in butter.

When the meat is tender, add some of the stock to the brown gravy; add the wine, spices, julienned and diced ingredients and cook about 10 minutes. To thicken the gravy, sprinkle some flour over it and mix. Slice the meat, pour the gravy over it, serve with potato croquettes. It can also be accompanied by mashed potatoes to which a little freshly grated horseradish has been added.

9.
Garnishings, Salads and Sauces

Besides the French and English style vegetable, Hungarian cooks often use potatoes, pasta, rice and dumplings, to accompany main dishes. We will give recipes of a few typical dishes which are the mainstay of the Hungarian cuisine.

76.
Stewed Sauerkraut

1.2 kg (5 cups) sauerkraut	pinch of paprika
30 g (3 Tbs) lard	————
50 g (½ cup) onion	100 g (⅔ cup) green pepper
5 g (1 tsp) paprika	50 g (1 small) tomato
garlic, caraway seeds	20 g (¼ cup) flour
————	1.5 dl (⅔ cup) sour cream
40 g (3 Tbs) lard	pepper
50 g (½ cup) flour	bunch of dill, savory

Prepare the sauerkraut according to Recipe 47.

Lightly brown the minced onion in the lard, add the paprika, stir, and add the sauerkraut. Brown it for a few minutes, then add water or stock to cover it; also add the crushed garlic and caraway seeds. To enhance a smoky flavor you may add bacon rinds, smoked meat or sausage. Be careful not to oversalt it. Cook covered until tender.

Meanwhile prepare a light brown roux from the lard and flour, stir in the paprika, add cold water, stir until smooth and pour over the sauerkraut. Add the diced green peppers and tomatoes; bring to a boil. Mix the flour and sour cream and stir into the boiling sauerkraut. Add to taste: salt, pepper and dill. This dish is often served as an accompaniment to smoked meat and sausage or with meat loaf or fried pork cutlets.

Garnishings, Salads and Sauces

77.
Boiled Cabbage

1.5 kg (3¼ lb) cabbage	50 g (½ cup) flour
salt, caraway seeds, pepper, garlic	40 g (⅓ cup) onion
20 g (2 Tbs) lard	———
80 g (3 slices) smoked bacon	30 g (¼ cup) flour
———	1.5 dl (⅔ cup) sour cream
40 g (3 Tbs) lard	parsley

Remove the core and shred the cabbage. Cook the cabbage partially in boiling stock or salted water. Add to the stock or water the caraway seeds, pepper and crushed garlic. Fry out the diced bacon in a very small amount of lard; add it to the cabbage. When the cabbage is almost done, prepare a light brown roux using the lard and flour and the finely chopped onion. Add cold water to the roux, stir until smooth, then stir it into the cabbage. Mix the flour and sour cream; stir into the cabbage. Boil briefly, then sprinkle with parsley. Stew for a while, making sure the cabbage is not overcooked.

This dish can be cooked and served with all kinds of smoked meat. It is often served as an accompaniment to *pörkölt,* lamb or mutton.

78.
Hungarian Steamed Cabbage

Instead of cabbage, sauerkraut can also be prepared this way.

1.8 kg (4 lb) cabbage,	60 g (½ cup) onion
red or white	caraway seeds
or a mixture of the two, salt	2 cl (2 Tbs) vinegar
100 g (½ cup) lard	1 dl (7 Tbs) wine
40 g (3 Tbs) sugar	or champagne

Remove the core and shred the cabbage. Salt it and let it stand for about half an hour, then squeeze well. In the lard lightly brown the sugar, add the finely minced onion and caraway seeds, brown, then add the cabbage and vinegar. Stew, stirring all the time, until all the liquid evaporates. Cover and continue cooking replacing the water as is needed. Instead of water, wine or champagne may also be used near the end of the cooking time. Do not overcook the cabbage; it should be crunchy.

This goes well with all kinds of *wurst,* roasted pork, goose or duck. If sauerkraut is used instead of cabbage (1½ kg/6⅓ cups), do not use vinegar and salt, but add 250 g (3 cups) of thinly sliced green peppers. This version is often served with breaded meat cutlets or other fried meats instead of a sour pickle.

79.
Braised Squash (Marrow)

2½ kg (5½ lb) yellow squash	60 g (½ cup) flour
or 1½ kg (3¼ lb) shredded squash	40 g (⅓ cup) onion
salt	20 g (¼ cup) flour
2 cl (2 Tbs) vinegar	2 dl (1 cup) sour cream
or lemon juice	15 g (1 Tbs) sugar
1 bunch of dill	20 g (2 Tbs) lard
40 g (3 Tbs) lard	pinch of paprika

Salt the shredded squash, let it stand for 20 minutes, squeeze dry, sprinkle vinegar over it. Chop the dill finely. Prepare a light roux of lard, flour and finely chopped onion, add ⅓ of the chopped dill and brown for 1 minute. Mix in the shredded squash carefully, brown it for a few minutes, then add a small amount of stock or water, stir until smooth and let it come to a boil. Mix the flour and sour cream and add, stirring, to the squash. Flavor with a small amount of sugar and vinegar to a piquant taste. In a small quantity of lard lightly brown the next ⅓ of the chopped dill and add to the squash. Do not overcook; shake the pot to prevent sticking. Before serving, sprinkle with the remaining ⅓ of the chopped dill and paprika.

Braised squash goes well as a side dish with meat loaf, *pörkölt,* roasts and grilled meat.

Garnishings, Salads and Sauces

80.
Stewed Green Beans

1.4 kg (3–3¼ lb) green beans	50 g (½ cup) flour
salt, garlic	20 g (3 Tbs) onion, parsley
30 g (2 Tbs) lard	3 g (1 tsp) paprika
30 g (¼ cup) onion	———
pinch of paprika	1.5 dl (⅔ cup) sour cream
———	2 cl (2 Tbs) vinegar
40 g (3 Tbs) lard	10 g (1 Tbs) sugar

Trim the green beans and cut into 2 cm (⅔ in) pieces. Cook in boiling stock or salted water with a crushed garlic clove. Lightly brown the onion in the lard, quickly mix in the paprika and pour into the cooking green beans. When the beans are almost tender, prepare a light roux from the lard and flour. Add the finely chopped onion, brown for another minute, add the chopped parsley, paprika and cold water, stir until smooth and add to the cooked green beans.

Mix the flour and sour cream and stir into the boiling green beans. Adjust the flavoring with vinegar or lemon juice and sugar until, the beans have a piquant taste. Serve with roasts, fried meat, meat loaf or *pörkölt*.

81.
Bean Stew

1 kg (2 ¼ lb) smoked meat	60 g (½ cup) flour
600 g (1 ¼ lb) kidney beans or	50 g (½ cup) onion
800 g (1 ¼ lb) fresh beans	3 g (1 tsp) paprika
bay leaf	1.5 dl (⅔ cup) sour cream
garlic	2 cl (2 Tbs) vinegar
30 g (2 Tbs) lard	10 g (1 Tbs) sugar

The day before you prepare this dish, cook the smoked meat until tender and let it cool in its own juice. Wash and soak the beans.

Next day, remove the accumulated fat from the top of the meat stock. Cook the beans in the soaking water enriched with some of the stock from the smoked meat. Use the rest of the stock in another dish. Add the bay leaf and crushed garlic to the cooking beans. Cook the beans under a lid until almost tender. Then, using the flour and the fat removed from the smoked meat (if necessary supplemented with some lard) prepare a light roux in 1–2 minutes. Add the finely chopped onion, lightly brown it, add the paprika, stir and add cold water to get a smooth roux. Stir into the cooked beans. Then add the sour cream. Flavor with a dash of tarragon vinegar and sugar, until a piquant taste is achieved.

This bean stew goes well with smoked meat, sausage and roasts.

This stew can also be puréed. Bean purée can be prepared without the roux and sour cream. In this case use white beans, cooked in the stock of the smoked meat with a bay leaf, garlic clove and 200 g (2 cups) chopped onion which should first be browned in the smoked lard. When cooked, drain and purée with the addition of some cooking liquid. Do not flavor with vinegar and sugar.

82.
Green Peas with Dill

1 bunch of tender dill	30 g (2 Tbs) lard or butter
30 g (2 Tbs) lard or butter	50 g (½ cup) flour
3 kg (6½–6¾ lb) unshelled	parsley
green peas or 1.2 kg (1½–1¾ lb)	1.5 dl (⅔ cup) milk
shelled green peas	40 g (3 Tbs) sugar
salt	2 g (dash) paprika

Chop the dill, stir half of it into the melted, hot shortening, add the green peas to the shortening, stir for 1–2 minutes, add salt and just enough stock or water to simmer the peas under cover. When the peas are partially cooked, prepare a light roux from the lard or butter and flour in about 1 minute; quickly add the remaining chopped dill, parsley, and cold milk, stirring until smooth. Add to the green peas. Flavor according to taste with sugar and a pinch of paprika. Bring to a boil once more. Green peas with dill go well with veal or poultry.

Garnishings, Salads and Sauces

83.
Lecsó (Green Pepper and Tomato Stew)

1.4 kg (3–3¼ lb) green peppers	80 g (6 Tbs) lard
600 g (1¼ lb) fresh tomatoes	50 g (2 slices smoked bacon)
150 g (1½ cups) onion	5 g (1 tsp) paprika, salt

Cut the green peppers lengthwise into slices, if hot, remove veins, if still hot, scald them. Poach the tomatoes for a few minutes in boiling water, peel them and cut into quarters. Cut the onion into rings, then cut the rings into halves.

Use a large saucepan, so the vegetables will not be too crowded. Dice the bacon and fry it out, then add the onion rings. Brown lightly. Quickly add the paprika, stir in the green peppers and tomatoes and salt. Cook first over high heat, then when most of the water has evaporated, cover and cook over medium heat until tender. (This amount is equal to approximately 1 kg (2¼ lb) preserved *lecsó*.)

Lecsó can be used either as a flavoring agent or a separate dish. If used as a meal, cook frankfurters or smoked sausages into the *lecsó* in one piece or in rings. Some people, just before serving, scramble an egg or two into the *lecsó*. Rice can also be cooked into *lecsó*. This will produce a more substantial meal.

84.
Pan-Cooked Potatoes with Paprika

2 kg (4½ lb) potatoes	salt
120 g (½ cup) lard	garlic, caraway seeds
180 g (1½ cups) onion	160 g (1 cup) green peppers
15 g (1 Tbs) paprika	80 g (medium) fresh tomato

Use potatoes which will not fall apart when cooked. Peel and cut the potatoes into longish segments. Brown the finely minced onion in the lard until golden yellow. Immediately add and stir in the paprika, the potatoes and some salt. Brown for a few minutes, then add water almost to cover the potatoes. Add garlic and caraway seeds to taste. Cover and simmer for about 8 minutes, then add the diced green peppers and tomato. If the potato will be served as a main dish, add smoked sausages or frankfurters and cook until the potatoes are done. Some people like this dish with more sauce; this can be achieved by adding more water or red wine to the potatoes during cooking.

85.
Potatoes Prairie Style

150 g (1 cup) carrots	40 g (3 Tbs) lard
120 g (1 cup) parsley roots	salt
60 g (½ cup) celery	10 g (2 tsp) paprika
1.5 kg (3¼ lb) potatoes	———
60 g (1 small) fresh tomato	salt
140 g (1 cup) green peppers	60 g (¼ cup) lard
80 g (¾ cup) onion	parsley

Dice the carrots, parsley roots and potatoes into small cubes, cut tomatoes to a larger size. Remove seeds from the green peppers and cut into rings.
Brown the finely minced onion to a light yellow color, add salt, carrots and parsley roots, stir and brown. Add the paprika, tomatoes and green peppers and simmer in stock or a small amount of water until tender. Cook the potatoes in a small amount of salted water, drain when done, and panfry in lard. Add the other vegetables, sprinkle with chopped parsley and carefully mix all ingredients together.
Prairie style potatoes may be served instead of other potato dishes as an accompaniment to any meat prepared without vegetables.

86.
Rice Batthyány Style

Named after Count Lajos Batthyány (1806–1849), who was Prime Minister of the first independent Hungarian government in 1848. He was executed when the war of independence failed. The difference between this version and the usual steamed rice recipe is that instead of water a dark consommé is used, which will impart a deep color and unique taste to the rice.

87.
Asparagus Hungarian Style

2 kg (4½ lb) asparagus, salt	6 g (1 tsp) paprika
10 g (2 tsp) sugar	salt
————	10 g (1 Tbs) sugar
50 g (1 cup) breadcrumbs	————
20 g (2 Tbs) butter	40 g (3 Tbs) butter
4 dl (1¾ cups) sour cream	80 g (6 Tbs) grated cheese
1 egg yolk	parsley

Cut the washed asparagus to 2–3 cm (1–1½ in) pieces or use only the tips. Cook the cut asparagus in salt water with a little bit of sugar until tender. Drain well. Brown the breadcrumbs lightly in butter. Mix the breadcrumbs into the sour cream, add egg yolk, paprika, salt and sugar and stir until smooth. Butter an oven-proof glass dish, place half the asparagus into the dish, pour ⅓ of the sour cream mixture over it, add the other half of the asparagus and all the sour cream mixture.
Sprinkle chopped parsley over the asparagus.
This dish can be served as an appetizer or with veal and poultry.

88.
Puréed Lentils with Poultry Liver

500 g (2½ cups) lentils	30 g (2 Tbs) lard
250 g (1¾ cups) diced liver	40 g (3 Tbs) flour
(chicken, duck or goose)	40 g (1 tsp) lard
5 cl (4 Tbs) red wine	5 g (6 Tbs) sugar
3 cl (2 Tbs) brandy	1 g (dash of) paprika
pepper, paté spices	15 g (1 Tbs) prepared mustard
————	15 g (1 Tbs) sugar
salt, bay leaf, garlic, savory	2 cl (2 Tbs) vinegar or lemon juice
————	10 g (2 Tbs) flour
40 g (⅓ cup) onion	1 dl (7 Tbs) sour cream
————	1 dl (7 Tbs) heavy cream

❋ Garnishings, Salads and Sauces ❋

The day before you want to cook the lentils wash and soak them. Dice the livers and marinate in the refrigerator. The marinade is made out of red wine, brandy, pepper and paté spices.

When you are ready to cook the lentils, add to the cooking water some salt, a bay leaf, and a small amount of garlic. Boil slowly until the lentils are tender, most of the cooking water should be absorbed. If you have stock from a ham, some of it can be used instead of water to enhance the flavor, but its taste should not become dominant.

Meanwhile lightly brown the minced onion in the lard, and cook the livers with the onion. In a small saucepan prepare a dark roux with lard and flour, add the sugar and brown together. This will produce a dark brown color. Add a pinch of paprika and cold water and stir until smooth. Stir the roux into the cooked lentils. Flavor with the mustard, sugar, vinegar or lemon juice. Finally, stir in the sour cream and flour mixture.

Use a food mill or a sieve to purée the liver and lentils. With a wire whisk mix the purées together. Bring to a boil whisking all the time; check the flavoring, adjust if necessary. Adjust the consistency of the purée by the addition of sweet cream. This purée is excellent with wild fowl. If you don't want to use liver, use 600 g (3 cups) lentils and a roux with minced onions. You may cook smoked meat or sausage into the lentils, or serve with beef *pörkölt*.

89.
Creamed Corn

1.2 kg (2¾ lb) corn on the cob or 600 g (3½ cups) tender corn kernels	*60 g (¼ cup) butter*
salt	*18 g (¼ cup) flour*
15 g (1 Tbs) sugar	*5 cl (¼ cup) white wine*
1.5 dl (⅔ cup) milk	*2 egg yolks*
2 dl (¾ cup) heavy cream	*1 dl (½ cup) heavy cream*

Use only young and freshly picked corn. Husk the corn, wash the corn on the cob and the husk. Use some of the husk to line the pot; cook the corn in salted water with a little bit of sugar added to it until tender. Remove the corn from the cob with a sharp knife. Try not to damage the kernels. Boil the kernels in the milk, butter and sweet cream. Knead the cold butter with the flour.

Crumble the butter-flour mixture over the corn, mix until thick and smooth, and add the wine. Boil once more. Let cool to about 80 °C (176 °F) and whisk in the cream mixed with the egg yolks. This is a good accompaniment to roast chicken or veal (for example, Recipe 59). If canned creamed corn is used, make sure it is not on the sour side.

90.
Egg Barley
(Tarhonya)

We discussed the origin of *tarhonya* in the Introduction. It is one of the oldest pasta foods used by the Magyar people. Very few people will make *tarhonya* at home today. We presume the reader will be able to find some imported from Hungary or buy the domestic type which is known as *egg barley*.

400 g (2⅓ cups) egg barley	100 g (½ cup) lard
50 g (1 small) fresh tomato	salt, 50 g (½ cup) onion
100 g (1 cup) green peppers	5 g (1 tsp) paprika

If the *tarhonya* is made with eggs, heat twice the volume of water; if you use an eggless variety, only 1½ times the volume of water is necessary. In another pot heat water to poach the tomatoes. Peel the tomatoes, remove the seeds from the green peppers and dice both.
In a large pot, heat the lard. Lightly brown the *tarhonya* over moderate heat and add the salt. Add and brown the finely chopped onions for 1–2 minutes, then quickly stir in the paprika and the hot water. Add the diced green peppers and tomatoes. Bring to a boil. Cover and cook in a medium hot oven without stirring for 20 minutes. When done, loosen the grains with a two-pronged fork, check it for flavoring and tenderness. It should be tender but not sticky and should fall apart into individual grains.
Tarhonya is served with *pörkölt, tokány* and *paprikás*.

91.
Galushka Dumplings

500 g (4⅓ cups) flour   salt
1 large or 2 small eggs   80 g (6 Tbs) lard

Sift the flour into a large bowl. Make a hollow in the middle of the flour, crack the eggs into the hollow and add salt and water in small portions while you beat the flour, eggs, and water with a wooden spoon into a semi-soft dough. The dough should easily come off the spoon.
Boil 3 liters (3 qt) of salted water in a large pot. Heat the lard in another saucepan. Use either a special utensil made to produce the small dumplings (similar to a food mill but with larger holes), or use a dampened chopping board and a wet knife. Cut the dough into strips, then into smaller pieces, and place into the boiling water. Some people, even members of the same family, have very different opinions about the correct size of the dumpling. It varies from the size of a small kidney bean to that of an unshelled peanut.
As the dumplings boil, they will come to the surface of the water. Remove them from the surface with a slotted spoon, rinse them and place them into the hot lard. Add the next portion of dumplings to the boiling water until all the dough is used up (about 3–4 cooking portions).
These tiny *galushka* dumplings are a must with the *paprikás, pörkölt* and *tokány*.

92.
Dill-flavored Cottage Cheese Dumplings

The preparation is similar to Recipe 104, but leave out the sour cream and buttered breadcrumbs. The quantities of the ingredients can be slightly reduced. On the other hand, add some pepper and half a bunch of finely chopped dill to the dough.
Before serving, wilt the other half of the chopped dill in 20–30 g (2 Tbs) butter and pour over the well drained large dumplings. Dill dumplings are often served with *paprikás,* or generally with meat dishes where the sauce contains sour cream, for example with chicken *paprikás*.

93.
Bayard Style Apples

Bring about ½ liter (1 pt) of water to a boil with some sugar, a cinnamon stick, clove, lemon peel (remove the white inner part) and 5 cl (3 Tbs) lemon juice. Peel 12 apples (Jonathans are very good for this dish) with a corrugated knife (for decoration). Remove the core, but do not cut all the way through: this hole will be stuffed. When an apple is peeled, drop it into the spicy water to prevent oxidation. Boil the apples until they are cooked but still firm. Remove with a slotted spoon and let cool. If apple preserve is used, just drain the apples.

While the apples are cooling mix cranberry or red currant jelly with slivered candied orange peel. Fill the center of the apples with the jelly and sprinkle a small amount of cinnamon over the apples. Chill well. Some people like to sprinkle a pinch of freshly grated horseradish over the apples. Other people use red (jaffa) orange slices, a larger one under and a smaller one above the apple for an effective decoration. Apples Bayard style are often served with hot and cold game or wild fowl dishes.

94.
Green Pepper Salad

Remove the cores from 900 g (2 lb) fleshy green peppers. If hot, remove the ribs also. Cut them into thin rings. Mince a small onion and sprinkle over the green peppers. Add salt and let stand for half an hour, stirring occasionally. Boil 2 dl (1 cup) water, cook the green pepper rings for 1–2 minutes under cover. Drain fast. If the cooking water is spicy hot and you want a milder flavor, do not use it for the dressing. Add to the water either vinegar or lemon juice, a little bit of sugar, some oil and salt; keep on tasting and adding until a piquant flavor is obtained. Pour the dressing over the green peppers and let them ripen in the refrigerator for 2–3 hours. Before serving, sprinkle chopped parsley over the salad and add a few slices of peeled tomatoes and black pepper to taste.

Garnishings, Salads and Sauces

95.
Fried Green Peppers with Mustard

Buy 12 large meaty green peppers. They should not be hot; use a reliable vendor. Clip the stem but do not puncture the peppers. Wash and dry them. Fry them in hot oil 2–3 peppers at a time, until the skin starts to get brown and blistery. Remove the peppers from the oil, peel off the outer thin skin while hot.

In a mixing bowl place 4 tablespoons of prepared mustard. Add black pepper, a small amount of sugar, lemon juice and tarragon leaves. Using the oil in which the green peppers were fried, prepare a dressing by whisking the oil into the mustard mixture. Taste it a few times to get the proper flavor, which should be spicy but not too hot. Dip the peeled fried peppers into the dressing until coated. Pour the rest of the dressing over the peppers; chill for 1–2 hours.

The left-over oil can be used for other salad dressings. It will impart a special flavor. Fried peppers with mustard go well with grilled meat. The taste might be sharp, but the guests (especially the men) will like it.

96.
Dill Gherkins

Use 1.8 kg (4 lb) medium-size kirby gherkins, a pickling variety. Cut off the two ends, taste to make certain that it is not bitter. Wash and slit the gherkins lengthwise, but do not cut them apart completely. Puncture the peel at a few places with the point of a knife. Wash a 5 liter (5 qt) glass jar, boil 2 liters (2 qt) of salted water in a degreased pot. Toast 150 g (5 slices) yeast bread. Place 1–2 slices of the toast in the jar, top it with fresh dill, 1–2 bay leaves, few peppercorns, 1 clove of crushed garlic and the gherkins. Finish the filling of the jar with more dill and a slice or two of the toast. Pour the cooled salted water into the jar to cover the gherkins. Seal the jar with cheese cloth or a sieve. Keep the jar in a sunny, but not too hot spot with even temperature for 5–6 days. The gherkins are ready when the color changes to a yellow green, the taste is crunchy and not too soft. Wash the gherkins, strain the milky looking pickling sauce back onto them and refrigerate. Dill gherkins should be consumed within 4–5 days. Serve over ice with a sprig of dill in its own pickling sauce. The sauce itself is very refreshing in hot weather. Serve with roasts and *pörkölts*.

Garnishings, Salads and Sauces

97.
Scalded Lettuce

4–6 heads of Boston	5 cl (4 Tbs) vinegar
or garden lettuce	or lemon juice
120 g (4 slices) smoked bacon	salt
15 g (1 Tbs) sugar	2 dl (¾ cup) sour cream (optional)

Wash and cut the lettuce. Fry out the diced bacon. Remove the bacon bits and keep them warm. Add to the dripping the vinegar, 2 dl (⅞ cup) water, salt, sugar, if you prefer a very small amount of crushed garlic, and bring the mixture to a boil. Pour over the lettuce and toss well. Serve topped with the bacon bits, and if you like, add some sour cream too.

98.
Gellért Salad

This was one of the specialities of the house in the Restaurant of the Hotel Gellért which was operated by Károly Gundel.

1.2 kg (2¾ lb) beets	3 cl (2 Tbs) lemon juice
5 cl (3 Tbs) vinegar	50 g (4 Tbs) French mustard
20 g (1 Tbs) sugar	cayenne pepper
40 g (3 Tbs) fresh horse-radish	Boston or garden lettuce
mayonnaise (Recipe 16) made out of	parsley
2 small eggs and	salt, caraway seeds
3.5 dl (1½ cups) oil	

The day before serving the salad, wash and cook the beets in salted water. Peel and slice them. Prepare ½ liter (2 cups) pickling sauce from water, vinegar, caraway seeds, a little bit of sugar and pieces of horseradish. Let the sliced beets stand in the sauce in the refrigerator overnight. Drain

XIII. Gundel salad

Garnishings, Salads and Sauces

the next day, julienne the beets and let them drip in a sieve. Prepare a thick mayonnaise, flavor it with mustard, lemon juice and cayenne pepper. Just before serving mix the beets into the mayonnaise. Line the salad bowl with lettuce leaves, arrange the beets on it, sprinkle it with chopped parsley and decorate with thin slices of peeled lemon.

Serve this salad with breaded cutlets, quick fries, veal or pork roasts. It also goes well with roast chicken and even with fish.

99.
Gundel Salad

300 g (4½ cups) small mushrooms
1 dl (7 Tbs) salad oil
salt, pepper, parsley
120 g (1 cup) very young string beans
200 g (about 8) asparagus tips
15 g (1 Tbs) sugar

150 g (1½ cups) green peppers
150 g (2 medium) fresh tomatoes
1 head of Boston or garden lettuce,
1 gherkin
5 cl (4 Tbs) lemon juice
ketchup (optional), parsley

Cut the mushrooms into segments and simmer in oil with salt and pepper and chopped parsley until tender. Cut the string beans to 1.5 cm (¾ in) pieces. Cook the beans and asparagus tips in salted water with a small amount of sugar. Poach the tomatoes, peel and dice. Fry the green peppers on a gridiron until the outer skin blisters up, pull off the skin and remove the core, then dice. Cut the two ends of the cucumber and taste to make sure it is not bitter. Peel and slice the cucumber very thinly; salt. Save a few large leaves of the lettuce and shred the rest of it. Let all the ingredients chill well. Drain the string beans and asparagus but not the mushrooms. Mix everything together, flavor with salt, pepper, lemon juice. (Ketchup is optional.) Let the flavor develop for an hour in the refrigerator. Serve on a bed of lettuce, decorated with sprigs of parsley. If you want to serve the Gundel salad as an appetizer, increase the quantities accordingly. Otherwise, serve it with meat.

XIV. Layered crepes

Garnishings, Salads and Sauces

100.
Károlyi Salad

The aristocratic Károlyi family produced writers, scholars, politicians, soldiers, landowners, and even a President of the Republic. We are not certain about which Károlyi this salad's name honors.

120 g (⅔ cup) dried white beans	2 egg yolks and
300 g (1¾ cups) potatoes	3½ dl (1½ cups) oil
150 g (2 cups) green peppers	for mayonnaise (Recipe 16)
300 g (1¾ cups) tomatoes	salt
120 g (¾ cup) dill gherkins	5 cl (3 Tbs) lemon juice
(Recipe 96)	pepper, cayenne pepper
3 hard-boiled eggs	40 g (scant 3 Tbs) prepared
2 heads of Boston or	mustard
garden lettuce	parsley

Cook the beans a day ahead. Slice the cooked and peeled potatoes thinly. Slice the cored green peppers, poached peeled tomatoes, peeled dill gherkins and hard-boiled eggs. Reserve 6 nice even slices of egg. Reserve a few nice lettuce leaves; shred the rest of the lettuce. Chill all the ingredients. Prepare a thick mayonnaise, flavor it using the spices. Drain the beans. Mix all the ingredients with enough dressing to coat well, but do not soak the vegetables. Serve decorated with the reserved leaves and egg slices, sprinkle with finely chopped parsley. This salad could be served as an appetizer or as an accompaniment to all kinds of meat dishes.

101.
Cold Red-Pepper Sauce

There are two variations: for the tastier, slightly sweet one, use 4 ripe red peppers. These will be available only for a short time in the growing season. Remove the core, grind the red peppers. Mix with salt, 30–40 g (2–3 Tbs) paprika and 1 dl (7 Tbs) dry red wine and freshly ground pepper. If red pepper is not available, for a substitute: boil 1½ dl (⅔ cup) salted water, mix in with a wire whisk 60 g (4 Tbs) paprika (a lot of people like to use hot paprika for this sauce). Keep on whisking the sauce until it begins to thicken. As it cools it will get thick; thin it to a thin tartar sauce consistency with dry red wine. Serve it with fatty and grilled meats.

102.
Csíki Sauce

120 g (⅔ cup) beets	1 dl (½ cup) white wine
80 g (⅔ cup) wine snap apple	50 g (3 Tbs) prepared mustard
1 bunch of chives	3 cl (2 Tbs) lemon juice
2 egg yolks and	10 g (2 tsp) sugar
3.5 dl (1½ cups) oil for	pepper, cayenne pepper
mayonnaise (Recipe 16)	salt, 1 dl (½ cup) sweet cream

The quantities are just an estimate; the exact amounts depend on the flavor of the apples, beets, and other ingredients. Add the flavoring in steps; taste often. The sauce should have a nice pink color, smooth texture, piquant taste and the flavors should blend properly.

Prepare the beets as in Recipe 98. Dice the beets and apples to 2 mm (⅛ in), chop the chives. Mix them into the thick mayonnaise, use the flavoring agents, if necessary add a little of the beet pickling sauce too. Use the cream as it is or whip it, and use the sugarless whipped cream to lighten the mayonnaise. Some people also add 60 g (½ cup) finely chopped braised mushrooms to the sauce.

This sauce can be used instead of tartar sauce or mayonnaise. Success is guaranteed.

10.
Desserts

On the menu of most Hungarian restaurants you can find internationally known desserts, all kinds of puddings, cakes and soufflés. Regional specialties like noodles Styrian style, bread, apple and jam pudding, and the like are also served. We shall not deal with these.

Our Austrian friends claim to be the "inventors" of the strudel. Possibly, but if so, surely they used the superior Hungarian flour for their strudel, wrote Károly Gundel.

We learned the basics of crepe-making from the French, but added a few of our own tricks to the art of delectable crepes. Noodles with cottage cheese, or other sweet toppings are not always a success with the international clientele, but it is among our favorites.

We will give the recipes for a few fancy pastries which were very popular at the Gundel restaurants. The Hungarian cheese recipes are also well received among our foreign visitors.

103.
Cottage Cheese Noodles

450 g (2 cups) cottage cheese	*10 g (1 Tbs) lard*
(not the sour type!)	*(add it to the water)*
600 g (4 cups) semolina flour	*50 g (¼ cup) lard*
4 eggs, salt	
5 g (1½ tsp) lard, salt	*120 g (6 slices) smoked bacon*
	3 dl (1¼ cups) sour cream, salt

Store the finely crumbled cottage cheese in a lukewarm place.

Mix the sifted flour with the salt, eggs and enough water to obtain a rather stiff dough. Work the dough until very smooth, form it into 3–4 balls. Oil the surface of the balls (use lard) and let them rest covered for 15 min. Roll each dough on a floured surface until very thin. Let it dry for a few minutes, then tear into 3–4 cm (1–1½ in) size noodles. Sprinkle with flour to prevent sticking, and air dry. In a pot boil 3 liters (3 qt) of salted water, adding a small amount of lard. Heat the rest

Desserts

of the lard in another 3 liter (3 qt) pot. In a frying pan fry the bacon bits (without their skin) and keep warm.

When the water boils, cook the noodles in 3 batches. Each batch should be well rinsed and allowed to drip before adding it to the melted lard. When all the noodles are cooked, mix in half the sour cream and cottage cheese. Heat up and pour into a preheated large bowl. Top with the rest of the not-too-cold cottage cheese and sour cream. Just before serving, pour the bacon bits and dripping over the noodles.

104.
Cottage Cheese Dumplings

800 g (3½ cups) cottage cheese	120 g (½ cup) lard
120 g (⅔ cup) farina	180 g (4 cups) breadcrumbs
salt	30 g (2 Tbs) butter
4 eggs	3 dl (1¼ cups) sour cream

These dumplings must be prepared just prior to serving. Force the cottage cheese through a sieve. Add the salt, farina and egg yolks. Mix all the ingredients together. Fold in the beaten egg whites carefully. Let the mixture rest for 50 minutes. Boil salted water in a large saucepan (18 dumplings should fit in one layer). For trial: form a dumpling 4–5 cm in diameter (2 in) with wet hands. Cook the dumpling in the boiling water until it comes to the surface (about 10–15 min). If the dumpling is too soft or falls apart, add a little bit more farina or flour; if it turns out to be too hard add some more cottage cheese. Cook the rest of the dumplings. Meanwhile melt the lard and lightly brown the breadcrumbs; then add the butter. Drain the dumplings with a slotted spoon, place them on a preheated platter, top them with the breadcrumbs and the lukewarm sour cream. Some people like to sprinkle confectioner's sugar on top of the dumplings or add some apricot jam. Others prefer the dumplings without the breadcrumbs or add salt instead of sugar.

Desserts

105.
Plum Dumplings

1.2 kg (2½–2¾ lb) potatoes, salt   *cinnamon powder*
300 g (2 cups) semolina flour   *80 g (⅔ cup) confectioner's sugar*
20 g (1 Tbs) lard   *salt*
1 large egg, salt

———   *180 g (4 cups) breadcrumbs*
400 g (14 oz) plums   *120 g (½ cup) lard*
(Italian or prune plums)   *20 g (2 Tbs) butter*

Cook the well washed potatoes (preferably the kind that falls apart during cooking) in salted water. Peel and mash them while still hot. When the potatoes are partially cooled, add the flour, lard, egg and a pinch of salt and mix into a dough. On a floured surface, roll the dough to ½ cm (⅓ in) thick and cut it to 5 x 5 cm (2¼ x 2¼ in) squares. Place a pitted plum in each square, and some cinnamon sugar in the place of the pit. Fold the corners over and form a ball; place the balls on a floured surface.

In a large saucepan, in which half the balls will fit in one layer, boil slightly salted water. Cook the dumplings in the boiling water over moderate heat until they come to the surface (10–15 min). Meanwhile lightly brown the breadcrumbs in the lard, and add some butter. Remove the dumplings from the water with a slotted spoon, let drain, then roll in the breadcrumbs. Sprinkle cinnamon and sugar over the dumplings and serve immediately.

Instead of plums, prune jam or apricot halves can also be used to fill the dumplings.

106.
Jam Pockets

300 g (1 cup) plum butter or plum jam
powdered cinnamon
20 g (2 Tbs) confectioner's sugar
———————
For the dough:
700 g (4¾ cups) semolina flour
3 eggs, salt
5 g (1 Tbs) lard (to coat)

1 egg (to close the pockets)
———————
120 g (½ cup) lard
20 g (2 Tbs) butter
180 g (4 cups) breadcrumbs
100 g (1 cup) confectioner's sugar
cinnamon powder
80 g (1 cup) walnut meal

Mix the plum butter or jam with the cinnamon sugar. You can add a little bit of plum brandy too. Prepare the dough according to Recipe 103 but using the ingredients listed above. Do not let the rolled dough dry. Place a teaspoonful of the jam every 5 cm (2¼ in) on the rolled dough. Make a grid with the well mixed egg between the jam. Cover it with another rolled dough sheet. Press the covering dough down on the egg lines with your fingers. Then cut along these lines with a pastry wheel. Cook the jam pockets in slightly salty water over medium heat, stirring occasionally. When the pockets come to the surface, remove and drain them well. Place half the breadcrumbs browned in the lard and butter into a flame-proof dish, put the pockets over the breadcrumbs. When all of them are cooked, cover them with the rest of the breadcrumbs. Carefully shake the dish or stir the pockets to coat them with the breadcrumbs. Mix the confectioner's sugar with the cinnamon and chopped nuts and sprinkle on top of the breadcrumbs.
The attentive host will have the lukewarm jam ready for those guests who might want it.

107.
Noodles with Ham

200 g (7 oz) ham or other
boneless smoked pork,
preferably a shoulder cut
————

For the noodles:
600 g (5¼ cups) flour
3 eggs, salt
3 g (1½ tsp) lard (for basting)
————

salt
10 g (1 Tbs) lard
————
80 g (6 Tbs) lard
3 eggs
2.5 dl (1 cup + 2 Tbs) sour cream
salt, pepper
15 g (1 Tbs) lard
15 g (⅓ cup) breadcrumbs

Cook and grind the not too lean meat. Prepare the noodles according to Recipe 103, cutting to 2 x 2 cm (¾ in) squares. Cook the noodles in salted water with a little bit of lard. Rinse and drain and mix the noodles together with the meat which should be prepared while the noodles are cooking. To prepare the meat, beat the egg yolk and lard together, add the sour cream and meat, adjust the flavor with salt and pepper, then fold in the beaten egg whites. Lightly grease a baking dish, sprinkle the breadcrumbs in it, put the meat-noodle mixture carefully into the pan and bake in medium hot oven until golden brown. Make sure the center is baked through. Cut into squares and serve.

108.
Simple Crepes
(9–12 pieces)

2 eggs
2 dl (¾ cup) milk
240 g (1½ cups) semolina flour

2 dl (¾ cup) milk or soda water
salt or sugar (optional)
100 g (½ cup) lard

XV. Strudel (with cheese, walnut and cabbage filling)

To obtain a very thin crepe mix the cold milk and eggs with a wire whisk, slowly add the flour and keep on mixing. When the dough is very smooth, add more milk or soda water until a cream-like consistency is obtained. If you wish to use a salty filling, as in Recipe 37, add a pinch of salt to the dough. If sweet filling is used, 10 g (1 Tbs) of sugar could be added but this will increase the risk of the crepe sticking to the pan. If the filling is sweet enough, don't add sugar to the dough.

Melt the lard in a small saucepan. Heat a well-cleaned crepe pan. Add ½ teaspoon of lard to the crepe pan and swirl to coat the pan. Pour the rest of the lard back into the saucepan. Pour about 1 dl (½ cup) dough into the hot crepe pan, swirl it around, fry over high heat, shaking the pan all the time. The dough should separate from the pan. Fry for 5 seconds longer, then turn and fry the other side too. If the crepe breaks or doesn't stay together, add an egg or flour to the mixture. If it is too thick, thin with soda water.

Stir the mixture before adding it to the hot crepe pan, otherwise the flour might settle out. If the crepe sticks to the pan the reason could be: 1) too much sugar; 2) either the pan or the lard was not hot enough or 3) the quantity of the lard was inadequate; 4) the crepe pan was not properly cleaned before or during the crepe making.

Several types of crepe filling are described in this book. For crepe with cottage cheese or walnuts use the simplified version of fillings in Recipe 110 or 109. Other variations follow.

108/a. Lemon-Flavored Crepes: Sprinkle the crepes with lemon juice, roll them up and sprinkle them with powdered sugar or powdered vanilla sugar. Serve lemon juice and sugar for additional flavoring.

108/b. Crepes with Jam: All kinds of jam can be used. In Hungary apricot jam is the favorite. The apricot jam can be flavored with apricot brandy (Recipe 123). If sour cherries are used, mix sugar and ground walnuts with the cherries.

108/c. Crepes with Coffee Filling: Use 36 g (½ cup) freshly ground coffee and add to it about 18 g (¼ cup) confectioner's sugar. Fill the crepes with the mixture. Fold and sprinkle confectioner's sugar on top of the crepes.

108/d. Crepes with Cocoa Filling: Instead of coffee use cocoa (Recipe 108/c).

XVI. Ewe-cheese spread

109.
Crepes Gundel Style

This is one of the most treasured creations of Károly Gundel. Unfortunately, the recipe is not followed faithfully in most places, including some of the Hungarian restaurants. Flambéing crepes can be a show stopper, but the process eliminates the necessary intense rum flavor from the walnut filling and chocolate syrup.

For the filling:	For the chocolate syrup:
1.5 dl (⅔ cup) rum	2.5 dl (1 cup+2 Tbs) milk
40 g (2⅔ Tbs) raisins	vanilla, 30 g (2 Tbs) sugar
20 g (2 Tbs) candied orange peel	————
180 g (1½ cups) chopped walnuts	100 g (½ cup) chocolate
1 dl (½ cup) heavy cream	1.5 dl (⅔ cup) heavy cream
120 g (½ cup) sugar	————
powdered cinnamon	3 egg yolks
————	80–100 g (6–7 Tbs) sugar
12 crepes	50 g (½ cup) cocoa
————	15 g (2 Tbs) flour
50 g (¼ cup) butter (for browning)	5 cl (4 Tbs) milk

Soak the raisins and finely slivered orange peels in rum for 24 hours. Grate the walnuts, but not too finely. Bring the cream to a boil, add the sugar, nuts, a pinch of cinnamon and drained raisins, the orange peel and cook it into a paste. (If necessary add a little milk.) Let the mixture cool partially and add half the rum. Make the crepes as in Recipe 108. Place the filling in a line on each crepe and roll it up. Keep the crepes warm.

For the sauce: boil the milk with the vanilla. Melt the chocolate in a small dish in the oven. Whip the heavy cream. With a wire whisk mix the flour and cocoa; add the cold milk and whip it until it is smooth and foamy. Mix in the melted chocolate, slowly whisk in the hot milk; heat to boiling point, but do not allow to boil. Remove from the heat and stir until it cools down somewhat. Carefully fold in the whipped cream and the remaining rum. The syrup should not be too sweet.

Some confectioner's sugar can be added if the chocolate is not sweet enough.

Brown the filled crepes in butter on both sides until they become crisp. Place them on a preheated flame-proof platter; pour the chocolate syrup over the crepes at the last minute before serving.

110.
Crepes Flambé with Cottage Cheese

30 g (2 Tbs) raisins	12 crepes (Recipe 108)
1.5 dl (⅔ cup) rum	———
———	20 g (1½ Tbs) butter
400 g (1¾ cup) cottage cheese	———
2 eggs, 120 g (⅔ cup) sugar	1 egg, 40 g (3 Tbs) sugar
30 g (2½ Tbs) vanilla sugar	2 dl (¾ cup) sour cream
½–1 dl (¼–½ cup) sour cream	———
lemon peel	50 g (½ cup) confectioner's
———	sugar

Soak the raisins in the rum for 24 hours. Push the cottage cheese through a fine sieve. Beat the egg white until stiff, but not dry. Cream the sugar and egg yolks until foamy, then beat in the vanilla sugar, sour cream and grated lemon peel. Add the cottage cheese and drained raisins; finally fold in the egg whites. Prepare 12 crepes according to Recipe 108. Place the filling in lines on the crepes, and roll them up. Butter a flame-proof platter and place the crepes in a single layer on the platter. Cream an egg with sugar, add the sour cream and pour the mixture over the crepes. Bake in a medium oven until lightly browned. Sprinkle sugar over the crepes. Partially heat the rum fortified with 96° alcohol. Pour over the crepes and ignite. Serve while the crepes are still burning. This filling can be prepared without sugar. Replace the raisins with finely chopped ham. Instead of vanilla use chopped dill. Instead of lemon juice black pepper can be used and salt should replace the sugar.

Desserts

111.
Crepes Filled with Cabbage

600 g (1¼ lb) cabbage   10 g (1 Tbs) sugar
salt   black pepper
40 g (3 Tbs) lard   12 crepes

Remove the core and shred the cabbage. Salt the cabbage and let it stand for a few minutes. Squeeze the cabbage dry. Brown the sugar in the lard. Mix the shredded cabbage into the lard and brown over moderate heat. Do not overcook.

In Recipe 108, omit the sugar. Instead of milk use soda water. Make the dough somewhat thicker than usual. Mix the cooked cabbage into the dough and make the 12 crepes.

As a variation, double the above ingredients. Make 12 regular crepes and fill them with the sautéed cabbage. Ground black pepper should be close at hand to flavor the crepes.

112.
Layered Crepes

Prepare the walnut filling according to Recipe 109, but reduce the walnut to 120 g (⅔ cup) and cut the other ingredients in the same proportion. Prepare the cottage cheese filling according to Recipe 110, use 180 g (¾ cup) cottage cheese and adjust the other ingredients also. Use 100 g (5 Tbs) apricot jam (Recipe 123) thinned with water so it will spread easily. Mix 50 g (½ cup) sifted cocoa with 30 g (¼ cup) confectioner's sugar.

Prepare 12 crepes according to Recipe 108. Butter a round flame-proof plate. Place the first crepe on it. Spread ⅓ of the walnut filling on the crepe. Place the next crepe over it and spread with ⅓ of the cottage cheese, spread the next crepe with ⅓ of the cocoa, and the next with ½ of the apricot jam. A little bit of melted butter can be also poured between the layers. Continue until all the crepes are used up. Do not fill the top one. Bake in moderate oven for 5–10 minutes. Beat 4–5 egg whites until stiff but not dry. Mix 100 g (3 Tbs) sugar and 50 g (2½ Tbs) apricot jam into the egg white. Spread the egg whites on the top of the layered crepes, as if frosting a cake. (A pastry bag can be used to produce a nicely decorated cake.) Brown the meringue in a medium hot oven for 3–4 minutes. Dip a knife into hot water to facilitate slicing. Sprinkle confectioner's sugar mixed with vanilla over each cake slice.

113.
Crepes Szentgyörgy Style

It is not very likely that this crepe is named after the Nobel-prize winner Dr. Albert Szentgyörgyi, who lives in the United States. Today's map of Hungary does not contain a community called Szentgyörgy, but the directory published in 1888 had 23 villages by this name. We presume that the original recipe comes from a town in Transylvania.

50 g (⅓ cup) raisins	150 g (⅔ cup) butter
1 dl (7 Tbs) rum	2 dl (¾ cup) heavy cream
———————	2 dl (1 cup) milk
20 crepes	———————
———————	100 g (1¼ cups) sugar
20 g (2 Tbs) butter	150 g (1¾ cups) almonds
———————	5 egg whites
120 g (½ cup+4 tps) sugar	100 g (½ cup) sugar
5 g (1 tsp) vanilla sugar	50 g (2½ Tbs) apricot jam
5 egg yolks	40 g (⅓ cup) confectioner's sugar

The ingredients listed above will be enough for 10 persons if the main course was substantial. Soak the raisins in rum for 24 hours. Increase the quantities in Recipe 108 by about 60 per cent to obtain about 20 crepes. Make a pile of 4 crepes and roll them up. Cut the ends straight. Butter a baking dish or round oven-proof dish. Cut the rolls so the length is about 1½ cm (¾ in) below the rim of the dish when they are stacked next to each other. The dish should be full but not crowded. Cream the egg yolks with the sugar and vanilla sugar until foamy, add the softened butter, sweet cream and milk. Mix it until creamy and smooth. Add to this the thinly sliced crepe ends, sugar, ground almonds and raisins. Pour this mixture over the crepes and bake in medium hot oven until the sauce jells. Meanwhile, whip the egg whites until stiff but not dry and flavor with sugar and apricot jam. Spread over the baked crepes. The meringue surface could be made wavy. Bake until the meringue is golden colored and sprinkle with confectioner's sugar. Cut it into even squares.
The crepes can also be flamed with lukewarm enriched rum.

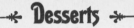
114.
Slipped Pancakes

This is really a cross between a pancake and a crepe, and the dough is different from Recipe 108.

60 g (¼ cup) butter, 6 eggs	*20 g (1½ Tbs) butter*
60 g (½ cup) confectioner's sugar	———
grated lemon peel	*120 g (1½ cups) ground walnuts*
120 g (1 cup) semolina flour	*120 g (1 cup) confectioner's sugar*
3–5 dl (1¾ cups) heavy cream	*200 g (¾ cup) orange marmalade*
———	*grated lemon peel*
80 g (6 Tbs) butter	*10 g (2½ tsp) vanilla sugar*
———	*vanilla*
For the punch sauce:	*2.5 dl (1 cup+2 Tbs) milk*
150 g (¾ cup) sugar	*8 cl (6 Tbs) rum*
3 egg yolks	*1 dl (7 Tbs) heavy cream*
10 g (2 Tbs) flour	

First prepare the punch sauce. Mix the sugar, egg yolks and flour with a wire whisk. Slowly whisk in the milk which was first scalded with the vanilla. Place over a low flame and bring to a boil while stirring continuously. Let cool slightly, add the rum and sweet cream, then add a few drops of red food dye to get a pink color. (Instead of the punch sauce, you can use chocolate sauce prepared according to Recipe 109.)

For the pancake dough: Cream the butter, egg yolks and confectioner's sugar. Add a small amount of grated lemon peel for flavor. Then while mixing slowly, add the flour and sweet cream. This should be a very smooth creamy dough. Fold in the stiff egg whites. Heat a small amount of butter in a crepe pan. Pour in dough to about the thickness of a pencil. Brown one side (do not turn). Butter a flame-proof platter and slide the pancake, soft side up, over to the platter. Sprinkle the slightly dried top side with a mixture of walnuts, sugar, and grated lemon peel. Add a few drops of orange marmalade too. Pile up the pancakes with the filling between them. The last pancake should be slipped on (hence the name) browned side up. Place in the oven for about 8 minutes. Sprinkle with confectioner's vanilla sugar. Cut in wedges and serve with the hot punch sauce served in a separate dish.

115.
Strudel Dough

350 g (3 cups) flour	10 g (2 tsp) lard to grease
25 g (2 Tbs) lard	the pan
1 large or 2 small egg yolks	30 g (2 Tbs) lard to sprinkle on
10 g (2 tsp) lard, vinegar	30 g (¼ cup) confectioner's sugar

Strudel can be made only from flour which has a high gluten content. Sift the flour onto a board. Make a depression in the center and in it place the lard, egg yolk, a few drops of vinegar and enough salted lukewarm water (about 2.5 dl, or 1 cup) to make a fairly soft dough. Work the dough until it peels off the board and starts to blister. Form the dough into a ball, grease lightly, place into a preheated bowl, cover the bowl and let the dough rest in a warm place for at least 20–25 minutes. Meanwhile prepare one of the strudel fillings. Cover a table, about 140 x 70 cm (56 x 28 in) size, with a clean tablecloth. (You must be able to walk around the table.) Place the dough in the center; clench your fists and place them under the dough, pulling the dough with your closed fists. The dough will stretch out evenly. Flour your fingers, walk around the table and stretch the dough by lifting and waving the edges. Be careful. Do it evenly so the very thin dough layer will not rip. If the edge of the dough sheet is thicker than the rest, remove it and re-use it after a resting period, stretching it as just described. If the dough will not stretch or rips, the fault is in the flour (or you need more practice). The dough sheet should cover the whole table and hang over. Most city stores today sell ready made strudel dough, which eliminates the tedious process of making your own. Let the dough dry for a few minutes, but not too long, otherwise it will become brittle. Sprinkle it with melted lard. The filling can be applied by two methods: 1) place the filling in a strip about 10 cm (4 in), working lengthwise; 2) evenly spread out the filling, leaving a 10–15 cm (4–6 in) empty border. We suggest using method 1) for cottage cheese or cabbage fillings, and method 2) for all other fillings. When the filling is distributed, fold the edges over filling and with the help of the tablecloth, roll up the strudel. Grease a cookie sheet, and cut the strudel to fit the cookie sheet lengthwise. Do not crowd the strudel rolls too tightly on the sheet. Sprinkle the top with melted lard and bake the strudels in a medium hot oven to a crisp light brown color. Sprinkle confectioner's sugar over the strudel with the exception of cabbage strudel.
Cut the strudel at an angle to get nice slices.

115/a. Fruit Fillings

1.5 (3¼ lb) fresh fruit	powdered cinnamon
60 g (1⅓ cups) breadcrumbs	30 g (3⅓ Tbs) raisins
120 g (1½ cups) ground walnuts	50 g (¼ cup) lard (for baking)
150 g (1¼ cups) confectioner's sugar	sugar

For apple strudel, winesnap apples are the best; definite use a tart apple. Peel and grate the apples. Sprinkle the breadcrumbs on the strudel dough, next add the grated apples evenly, follow it with the ground walnuts, raisins, sugar to taste and cinnamon. Roll it up fairly tightly and bake it. Other often used fruit fillings are pitted cherries, sour cherries or a mixture of the two. Pitted plums are also used. With these fruits omit the raisins. If not-too-ripe strawberries are used, increase the amount of breadcrumbs in the recipe.

115/b. *Walnut Filling:* Use more lard to moisten the rolled out strudel dough. Sprinkle on: the breadcrumbs, 360 g (4½ cups) ground walnuts, 200 g (1 cup) sugar, 60 g (6⅔ Tbs) raisins and some grated lemon peel, then roll up the dough.

115/c. *Almond Filling:* Sprinkle 60 g (1⅓ cups) breadcrumbs on the strudel dough, spread 180 g (9 Tbs) currant or raspberry jam on the dough. In a mixing bowl cream 4 egg yolks, 180 g (6 oz) of sugar, add 40 g (⅓ cup) flour, and 3 dl (1¼ cups) milk to it, mix in 300 g (3¾ cups) almonds and bring it to a boil. Fold in the stiff egg whites and spread the mixture on the strudel dough. Roll it up and bake it.

115/d. *Cabbage Filling:* Increase 2.5 times the quantity of the filling in Recipe 111 (1.5 kg (3¼ lb) cabbage). Sugar is omitted of course.

115/e. *Poppy Seed Filling:* Grind 360 g (¾ lb) poppy seeds, add them to 3 dl (1¼ cups) milk, 300 g (3 cups) confectioner's sugar and some grated lemon peel, cook this mixture until it has a spreading consistency. Now add to the mixture 60 g (6⅔ Tbs) raisins and 200 g (2 cups) peeled grated apples. Sprinkle 60 g (1⅓ cups) breadcrumbs on the strudel dough, then spread the poppy seed–apple mixture over it.

115/f. Chocolate Filling: Boil together 2 dl (1 cup) milk, 2 dl (¾ cup) sweet cream, 120 g (½ cup) vanilla sugar. Whisk in 60 g (½ cup) cocoa. Remove it from the heat, mix in 3 egg yolks, 30 g (3⅓ Tbs) raisins, 50 g (¼ cup) butter, 50 g (¾ cup) almonds. Instead of breadcrumbs, sprinkle 60 g (8 pieces) crushed *zwiebacks* over the stretched strudel dough before spreading the above mixture over the dough. Grate 80 g (3 squares) chocolate over the filling before rolling it up.

115/g. Cottage Cheese Filling: For this filling, increase the quantity of the ingredients by 50 per cent in Recipe 110.

116.
Cobbler's Delight

For the noodles:	For the strudel dough:
250 g (2¼ cups) semolina flour	250 g (2¼ cups) flour, vinegar
2 eggs, salt	15 g (1 Tbs) lard, 1 egg yolk
2 g (½ tsp) lard	5 g (1½ tsp) lard

For the filling:	Miscellaneous:
200 g (1 cup) vanilla sugar	10 g (2 tsp) lard (for the water)
100 g (½ cup) butter, 4 eggs	20 g (2 Tbs) lard (to grease the pan)
600 g (2½ cups) cottage cheese	50 g (¼ cup) butter
5–6 dl (2–2½ cups) sour cream	(to sprinkle on the dough)
60 g (7 Tbs) raisins	40 g (3 Tbs) vanilla sugar
lemon peel	(for topping)

Follow Recipe 103 and use the list of ingredients to make the noodle dough. Let the dough rest while it is slightly greased, then roll it out very thin and cut it into fine noodles. Cream the butter, egg yolks and vanilla sugar until foamy. Add the fine-curd cottage cheese, sour cream, raisins and grated lemon peel to the creamed butter and mix it together. Boil water to cook the noodles. Follow Recipe 115 and use the list of ingredients to make the strudel dough. While this dough is resting, cook the noodles in slightly salted water, add a bit of lard to the water. Mix together the well-drained noodles and the cottage cheese mixture, fold in the beaten egg whites. Stretch out the strudel dough, let it dry for a few minutes, place 3 layers of strudel dough in a well greased baking

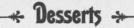

pan, sprinkling butter between the layers. Pour the cottage cheese mixture over the strudel dough, cover it with another 3 layers of dough. Sprinkle the top with melted butter and bake it in a medium hot oven. Make sure that the center is cooked well, and the top is crisp (about 25 min.). Let it settle for 10–12 minutes, cut it to 6 squares, sprinkle with confectioner's sugar and serve.

117.
Rigó Jancsi

Named after the gypsy violinist Jancsi (John) Rigó (?–1927), who seduced and married the wife of the Belgian prince Chimay. The sensational marriage with an American millionnaire's daughter did not produce an offspring, but the world gained a delicious pastry. The ingredients below are enough for about 20 servings.

4 eggs, separated	100 g (3½ squares) baking chocolate
30 g (¼ cup) confectioner's sugar	———
50 g (½ cup) confectioner's sugar	6 dl (2½ cups) heavy cream
100 g (7 Tbs) melted butter	50 g (½ cup) confectioner's sugar
80 g (¾ cup) flour	———
20 g (3 Tbs) cocoa	30 g (1½ Tbs) apricot jam
5 g (1 Tbs) flour (to sprinkle)	150 g (⅔ cup) chocolate fondant

Cream the egg yolks and 30 g (¼ cup) confectioner's sugar. Whip the egg whites with the 50 g (½ cup) confectioner's sugar until stiff. Add the mixture to the creamed egg yolks fold in the melted butter and mix in the flour and cocoa.

Cover a baking sheet with buttered parchment paper and spread the above mixture about 1.5 cm (¾ in) thick on it. Bake it in a 200–220 °C (400–425 °F) oven. When the cake is done, sprinkle the flour on top and turn it out on a board. Pull the paper off and let the cake cool.

Melt the baking chocolate in a double boiler. Boil and cool the heavy cream before whipping the cream and sugar to make whipped cream. Mix a small amount of the whipped cream into the warm chocolate, then fold in the rest of it lightly. Cut the cake into half. Spread one half lightly with jam, then cover with the chocolate fondant. When the fondant has cooled down, cut the cake to 5x5 cm (2½x2½ in) squares. Spread the chocolate whipped cream on the other half of the cake, then place the fondant covered squares tightly on top. Refrigerate the cake well, then cut around the squares with a knife which has been dipped into hot water and dried.

118.
Cottage Cheese Pastry Rákóczi Style

This pastry was created by Chef János Rákóczi (1897–1966).

For the dough:	For the fillings:
180 g (1½ cups) flour	600 g (2½ cups) cottage cheese
120 g (½ cup+1 Tbs) butter	2 dl (¾ cup) sour cream
60 g (½ cup) confectioner's sugar	40 g (4½ Tbs) raisins
1 dl (7 Tbs) sour cream	grated lemon peel
2 egg yolks	——
baking soda or baking powder	2 egg whites
For the topping:	30 g (2 Tbs) cookie crumbs
120 g (1 cup) confectioner's sugar	3 egg whites
30 g (2 Tbs) vanilla sugar	90 g (¾ cup) confectioner's sugar
3 egg yolks	red currant or apricot jam

Prepare the dough from the flour, butter, sugar, sour cream, egg yolks and a ¼ teaspoon of baking soda or baking powder. When the dough is formed into a ball, let it rest for a while. Then roll it out to the size of the baking pan, line the pan with the dough; sprinkle the dough and bake it until partially done.

Meanwhile beat the egg yolks with the sugar and vanilla sugar until light and foamy, add the cottage cheese, sour cream, raisins, grated lemon peel, and mix it all together. Finally fold in the beaten egg whites.

Sprinkle the dough with the cookie crumbs, and spread the cottage cheese mixture evenly over the dough. Bake it in a moderate oven. Beat the rest of the egg whites until stiff and mix in the confectioner's sugar. When the pastry is almost ready, with the help of a pastry bag draw a trellis over the pastry with the meringue; bake it until the meringue is golden brown. Fill the spaces between the meringue lines with the jam. Let the pastry cool for a while before cutting it into squares with a wet knife.

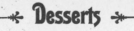

119.
Sponge Cake Somló Style

This delectable dessert is the creation of Károly Gollerits, who was the Maître d'hôtel of the City Park Gundel Restaurant for 16 years. The ingredients below are for 10–12 servings.

For the topping:	*100 g (½ cup) sugar*
100 g (1 cup) walnuts	*½ dl (4 Tbs) milk, 1 vanilla bean*
80 g (½ cup) raisins	*For the syrup:*
1 dl (7 Tbs) rum	*200 g (1 cup) sugar, 0.3 dl (2 Tbs) water*
For the sponge cake:	*15 cl (⅔ cup) rum*
8 eggs 160 g (1½ cups) flour	*lemon or orange peel*
160 g (¾ cup) sugar	———
40 g (7 Tbs) walnuts	*20 g (3 Tbs) cocoa, 80 g (4 Tbs) raspberry*
20 g (3 Tbs) cocoa	*or apricot jam*
For the vanilla cream:	*300 g (1¼ cups) sweet cream*
4 egg yolks, 30 g (¼ cup) flour	*3 portions (6 Tbs) of chocolate syrup*

Soak the raisins in the rum and grind the walnuts a day ahead of time.

To prepare the sponge cake: Beat the egg whites in the mixing bowl, slowly add the sugar, beat it until stiff, stir in the egg yolks, then the flour. Divide the dough into 3 parts, into the first ⅓ mix in 40 g (½ cup) ground walnuts, into the second ⅓ mix in the cocoa, the third portion remains plain sponge cake. Bake the ginger-thick cake layers in a steam-free medium hot oven.

For the vanilla cream: scald the milk with the vanilla bean, add the egg yolks, sugar and flour, and to be on the safe side, add a small amount of gelatin.

For the syrup: cook the sugar for 15 min. in the water, which is flavored with the lemon and orange peel. When the syrup is cool, add the rum. To assemble the cake, the bottom layer is the walnut flavored sponge cake. Sprinkle it with ⅓ of the syrup, spread ⅓ of the walnuts and raisins over it, and ⅓ of the vanilla cream over the walnuts. The middle layer is the cocoa flavored sponge cake, then repeat the filling process. The top is the plain sponge cake which is sprinkled with rum, then the jam is spread over it before the vanilla cream is added. Sprinkle the top with cocoa. Refrigerate the cake for a few hours.

Desserts

Serving can be either by cutting the cake into squares and placing the squares on individual glass dishes or by scooping tablespoon size "dumplings" out of the cake. Top the cake with whipped cream and with thick chocolate syrup (Recipe 109).

120.
Gellért's Parfait Bomb
For 10 portions

This dessert is named after the Gundel restaurant once located in the Hotel Gellért.

For the cranberry or raspberry and vanilla ice cream:
12 dl (5¼ cups) heavy cream
150 g (½ cup) cranberry or raspberry jam

80 g (⅔ cup) confectioner's sugar
15 g (2 envelops) gelatin
250 g (1 cup) brandied cherries

2 dl (⅞ cup) milk
⅓ of a vanilla bean
2 egg yolks
80 g (⅔ cup) confectioner's sugar
20 g (¼ cup) flour

10 portions (1¼ cups)
of chocolate syrup

40 g (⅓ cup) confectioner's sugar,
4 g (1 tsp) vanilla sugar

The bomb mold is turned upside down and lined with the strongly flavored soft cranberry or raspberry parfait. Make sure that when parfait is prepared the pits and peels of the fruit are removed. Fill the rest of the mold with soft vanilla ice cream, except the center where a tapered water glass is placed to create a cavity. Freeze the parfait. Remove the glass and fill the cavity with the brandied cherries which are soft-jelled by the addition of gelatin. Return the mold to the freezer. When it is completely frozen, dip the mold in hot water, place a glass platter over it and turn the mold out onto the platter. Decorate the bomb with whipped cream. When the bomb is cut, the surprise is the brandied cherry filling. The hot chocolate syrup which is served over the individual portions creates a surprising taste. You can serve a wafer or plain cookie with parfait bomb.

❈ Desserts ❈

121.
Plum Pastry

For the pastry:	For the filling:
100 g (½ cup) sugar	*80 g (1 cup) ground walnuts*
200 g (¾ cup) butter	*1 kg (6 cups) pitted plums*
300 g (2½ cups) flour	*(Italian or prune plums)*
1 egg yolk	*120 g (1 cup) blanched*
10 g (2 tsp) vanilla sugar	*slivered almond cinnamon powder*
grated lemon peel	*80 g (6½ Tbs) sugar*
10 g (2 tsp) baking powder	

Make a dough from the listed ingredients using 2 tablespoons of water. Roll out to about 4 mm (⅜ in) thickness and place it in a baking pan. Bake until the top starts to get brown and puffy. Sprinkle the ground walnuts over the partially baked dough. Place the plum halves, cut side up, over the walnuts. Spread the blanched almond slivers over the plums. Sprinkle the sugar and cinnamon over the almonds and bake in a 140 °C (275 °F) oven (if you have a top flame in the oven, use that), for about 20 minutes. This pastry is very good served warm or cold.

122.
Stuffed Cantaloupe

Cut into halves 3 small ripe cantaloupes, discard the seeds, remove with a teaspoon about ⅓ of the cantaloupe. Sprinkle some confectioner's sugar on the cantaloupes, then pour 1 cl (1 Tbs) brandy into each half, pricking the flesh at a few places. Refrigerate the cantaloupes.
Rub sugar cubes over well washed orange rinds, pour 5 cl (4 Tbs) Triple Sec and 5 cl (1 Tbs) maraschino liquor over the sugar cubes, and mash them with a fork. Add the spooned out cantaloupe pieces to the sugar, along with 4–5 other kinds of fresh fruit. If fruits are not in season, use preserves. Mix in with the fruits about 120 g (1 cup) chopped walnut pieces; flavor the fruit salad further with lemon juice. Let it stand in the refrigerator for 1–2 hours for the flavors to blend. Prepare 6 dl (2 ½ cups) fruit ice cream. The kind depends on the fruit used in the fruit salad: do not duplicate; the fruits and ice cream should be complimentary. The possibilities are lemon, strawberry, raspberry, or raisin-punch ice cream. Just before serving, place some of the ice cream

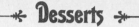

in the partially scooped out cantaloupes and top with the fruit salad. Whipped cream can be used as decoration. Serve plain cookies or wafers with it. Do not add too much sugar to the cantaloupes; rather, place a dish of extra sugar on the table.

123.
Brandied Apricot Jam

This could be used instead of a syrup or sweet sauce over crepes, or puddings or over a somewhat dry pastry. Cook the apricot jam with enough water to make it soft. When it cools down, mix 5 cl (3 Tbs) apricot brandy to 300 g (1 cup) jam.

124.
Ewe-Cheese Spread

450 g (1 lb) ewe-cheese	*20 g (4 tsp) paprika*
200 g (¾ cup) butter	*caraway seeds, beer*
about 30 g (2 Tbs) mustard	*1 bunch of chives*
2 sardines or the oil from a can of sardines	*10 capers*

Press the ewe-cheese through a sieve. Mix it well with the butter, mustard, sardines (or sardine oil, or use anchovy paste), paprika and caraway seeds. If the spread is not soft enough, add a small amount of beer. Add the finely chopped chives and capers to taste.
Serve with fresh radishes, green peppers or scallions; some people like slivers of garlic with it. This spread goes well with wine.
The spread, known as *körözött* in Hungary, can be used to stuff cored green peppers. After the stuffed peppers are chilled, slice them with a knife which has been dipped in hot water. Serve the spread at room temperature; the taste and texture is much better this way than when it is chilled.

Postscript

We say farewell to our readers with quotations from the elder Gundel and his two sons:

KÁROLY GUNDEL: "The modern trend in music is the creation of cacophony, random mixture and the dissolving of sounds, the emphasis of rhythm over melody,... the search for exotic effects. Gastronomy as a form of art is searching for harmony in both the preparation of dishes and the selection of menus... and in this coincides with musical trends only in that it searches for novelty." (1934)

IMRE GUNDEL described it rather similarly. "It is great luck that gastronomy is the most conservative of the arts. We are not looking for novelty for its own sake, for the bizarre, for the cacophony of flavors, for the disharmony of colors. In the province of taste we are not following the often hair-raising and disquieting trends of the various 'isms'.
A chemist friend of mine always said: 'If I carry a flask from one place to another and worry about what would happen if the flask would break, I'm sure I'd stumble on a strand of hair.' The same applies to cooking: You should not be afraid. You should work with ease, follow general rules and specific instructions; if you make a mistake, you can correct it with a little inventiveness. My other advice is: Don't neglect the final flavoring. I usually taste food which contains sugar, salt, vinegar 6–8 times; after boiling I add this or that flavor. Taste the food carefully, like a painter who checks his work from many angles."

FERENC GUNDEL: "My dear mother used to stand in the circle of stoves, tasting the various dishes. She'd add a few drops of lemon juice, a few grams of herbs, a little butter, cream, or cognac. I am convinced that just these few drops and grams raised the fame of Gundel, and through it, the prestige of the Hungarian Cuisine.
If with the help of this little book you will have success in your home, remember that the real Hungarian flavors are best enjoyed in Hungary. The Hungarian catering trade is waiting for you with the friendliness of amateurs and with the preparedness of professionals.
Until we can see you in person, in our thoughts we raise a glass of *Tokay Aszu*, 'the King of wines and the wine of kings,' to your health, and to the health of your family, and we welcome you as a new member into the ever expanding society of the white table." (1983)

Corvina Kiadó